HANDBOOK

OF THE

RUSSIAN TROOPS IN ASIA.

Prepared in the Intelligence Division of the War Office

BY

MAJOR J. WOLFE MURRAY, R.A., D.A.A.G.

The Naval & Military Press Ltd

Published by the
The Naval & Military Press

Unit 10 Ridgewood Industrial Park,
Uckfield, East Sussex, TN22 5QE
Tel: +44 (0) 1825 749494
Fax: +44 (0) 1825 765701

MILITARY HISTORY AT YOUR FINGERTIPS
www.naval-military-press.com

ONLINE GENEALOGY RESEARCH
www.military-genealogy.com

ONLINE MILITARY CARTOGRAPHY
www.militarymaproom.com

In reprinting in facsimile from the original, any imperfections are inevitably reproduced and the quality may fall short of modern type and cartographic standards.

PREFACE.

A PREVIOUS handbook has given the details of organisation, &c., of the Russian Army in Europe. In it the reserve formations were omitted, but in this handbook the reserve and local troops have been included, so that a comprehensive idea of the Russian military system in Asia may be formed. Part of the matter of the previous handbook has here been reproduced, to make this work complete in itself.

H. BRACKENBURY,

D.M.I.

Intelligence Division,
War Office,
March, 1890.

CONTENTS.

PL. I

Shoulder Strap.

PRIVATE

of the 4th Turkestan rifle battalion

Int. Div. No 780 a.

Litho at the Intell. Div W.O. Nov 1889.

PL. II.

Shoulder Strap.

COSSACK

of the 5th Orenburg regiment.

Int. Div. No. 780 b. Litho at the Intell. Div. W.O. Jany 1880

PL. III.

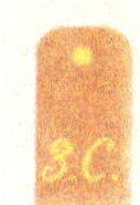

Shoulder Strap.

GUNNER

of the 2nd field battery

West Siberian artillery brigade.

Int. Div. No 780. c. *Litho. at the Intell. Div. W.O. Dec. 1889*

CHAPTER I.

ORGANISATION AND STRENGTH.

TRANSCASPIA.

THE boundaries of the Transcaspian province may be roughly stated as follows: on the west the Caspian Sea; on the south the Russian frontier from the Caspian to the Oxus; on the east the Oxus; and on the north a line running from the south of the Sea of Aral to Mertvy Kultuk Bay on the Caspian.

The head-quarters of the province are at Askabad, the residence of the Governor and Commander-in-Chief. This officer enjoys a certain degree of independence, though nominally a subordinate of the Governor-General of the Caucasus.

ORGANISATION.

The following troops are quartered within the limits of the command (*vide* p. 62).

Field troops.

Infantry—2 bdes. Transcaspian rifles, of 4 bns. each.
Cavalry—1 bde. of 2 Cossack regts., of 6 sqns. each; 3 sqns. Turkoman Militia.
Artillery—2 field, 1 mountain, 1 horse, batteries.
Engineers—1 company.

Railway troops.

2 railway battalions.

Local troops.

Infantry—7 local detachments.
Artillery—1 fortress company.

STRENGTH.

Infantry.—The infantry consists of rifles organised in brigades, each comprising 4 battalions of 4 companies each. The battalions are numbered consecutively from 1 to 8. The war strength of the units is practically as below :—

A company = 4 officers, 240 combatants.
A battalion = 21 „ 960 „

The battalion has in addition a non-combatant section of 4 officials and 56 rank and file with 43 horses.

In peace these troops are maintained at a high figure, so that only a small accession to their strength is necessary to enable them to take the field in full force, the peace establishment being—

A company = 3 officers, 200 combatants.
A battalion = 17 „ 800 „

Cavalry.—The cavalry brigade consists of the Taman and Kavkaz regiments, of Kuban Cossacks, each of 6 squadrons, with the following effective both in peace and war.

Squadron = 3 officers, 144 combatants, 147 horses.
Regiment = 22 „ 867 „ 893 „

The regiment has in addition a non-combatant section consisting of 5 officials, 109 rank and file, and 159 horses.

The 3 squadrons of Turkoman Militia, which are employed mainly on detached and cordon duties, amount to 5 officers and 310 rank and file.

Artillery.—The following batteries are quartered within the command :—

4th light field battery, 20th brigade.*
3rd light field battery, 21st brigade.*
6th mountain battery, 21st brigade.*
4th horse artillery battery Kuban Cossacks.

The war strength of these batteries is as below :—

Batteries.	Officers.	Men.		Horses.	Guns.
		Combatant.	Non-combatant.		
Light field	6	205	22	181	8
Mountain	6	233	67	216	8
Horse artillery ...	5	204	33	252	6

In peace these batteries are maintained very nearly at the war strength, with the exception of the Cossack battery, which would require an addition of about 70 horses. The batteries maintain all their guns, and about two ammunition wagons each, fully horsed during time of peace.

Engineers.—The Transcaspian sapper company has a strength of 7 officers, 259 combatants, 22 non-combatants, and 30 horses in peace and war.†

A railway battalion has a strength in peace and war of 27 officers and officials, 995 combatants, and 40 non-combatants, with 69 horses. The two battalions are employed in working the Transcaspian railway.

Local detachments are maintained as follows :—

Alexandrovsk (248), Askabad (365), Chikishliar (186,) Duz-olum (104), Krasnovodsk (189), Merv (186), Sarakhs (244).

* The artillery brigades, from which these batteries are detached, are quartered in Cis-Caucasia.

† The company comprises a small telegraph and heliograph detachment, which on mobilization requires 62 additional horses.

Fortress artillery.—The Askabad company consists of 4 officers and 110 men.

The strength of all ranks on the peace and war footings is given below :—

	Field Troops.					Railway Troops.	Local Troops.		Grand Total.	
	Infantry.	Cavalry.	Artillery.	Engineers.	Total.		Infantry.	Artillery.	Men.	Guns.
Peace...	6,818	2,325	945	288	10,376	2,124	1,522	115	14,137	30
War ...	8,321	2,325	1,014	288	11,948	2,124	1,522	115	15,709	30

About 400 horses will be required to be obtained to complete the force to war strength.

TURKESTAN.

The boundaries of the Turkestan military district may be roughly described as follows :—

On the south a line drawn from Lake Karakul in the Pamir, to Khoja Saleh on the Oxus (thus including the territory of Bokhara in the district) ; on the west the course of the Oxus and the east coast of the Aral Sea ; on the north a line joining the northern angle of the Aral Sea with the southern extremity of Lake Balkhash ; on the east, a line drawn from the southern extremity of Lake Balkhash to Lake Karakul.

Tashkend is the seat of the head-quarters of the district, both military and political, and the Governor-General and Commander-in-Chief resides there.

Organisation.

The troops quartered in the district consist of (*see* p. 63).

Field Troops.

Infantry—1 bde. Turkestan rifles, 4 bns.
20 bns. Turkestan frontier troops.
Cavalry—3 regts. Orenburg Cossacks, 4 sqns. each
1 regiment of Ural Cossacks, 4 sqns.
2 sqns. Astrakhan Cossacks.
Artillery—Turkestan bde., 7 batts., 8 guns each.
2nd Orenburg horse batty, 6 guns.
1 mountain horse batty, 6 guns.
Engineers—Turkestan Sapper half-battalion.

Local Troops.

Infantry—12 local detachments.
Artillery—2 fortress companies.

Strength.

Infantry.—The rifle brigade consists of 4 battalions, numbered 1 to 4, each of 4 companies. The frontier battalions, numbered 1 to 20, are grouped arbitrarily into 4 brigades according to the districts in which they are quartered; but this arrangement is mainly for administrative purposes.

The strength of the units is as shown below :—

Rifle	Company	Peace	3 officers,		200 combatants.
		War	4	,,	240 ,,
	Battalion	Peace	17 officers,		800 combatants.
		War	21	,,	960 ,,
Frontier	Company	Peace	3 officers,		170 combatants.
		War	4	,,	240 ,,
	Battalion	Peace	17 officers,		680 combatants.
		War	21	,,	960 ,,

In addition each battalion has a non-combatant section of 3 officials, 56 to 60 rank and file, and 35 to 43 horses.

Cavalry.—The cavalry consists of the 4th, 5th, and 6th regiments of Orenburg Cossacks, the 2nd regiment of Ural Cossacks, each of 4 squadrons, and of 2 squadrons of Astrakhan Cossacks.

The strength of these troops in peace and war may be stated in round numbers as :—

Squadron = 3 officers, 148 combatants, 150 horses.
Regiment = 15 „ 600 „ 610 „

The regiment has, in addition, a non-combatant section of 3 officials, 75 non-combatants, and 105 horses.

Artillery.—The Turkestan brigade consists of 7 batteries, Nos. 1 to 7. Nos. 1 and 2 are heavy field, Nos. 3 to 6 are light field*; and No. 7, a mountain battery. There are also the 2nd Orenburg Cossack horse battery, and the Turkestan mountain horse battery.

The establishments of these batteries is as below :—

Battery.		Officers.	Rank and File.		Horses.		Guns.
			com-batant.	non-combat-ant.	Peace.	War.	
Turkestan brigade	heavy, No. 1 ...	6	236	22	140	207	8
	heavy, No. 2 ...	6	236	22	50	207	8
	light, Nos. 3–6 ...	6	204	22	140	181	8
	mountain, No. 7 ...	6	233	67	72	206	8
Cossack		5	180	29	154	242	6
Mountain horse		5	181	54	141	241	6

In addition depôt divisions are maintained, of 46 men for the 1st heavy battery, of 38 men for the light batteries.

* Nos. 3 and 4 batteries though denominated as, and having an establishment of personnel for, light field batteries, are armed with the horse artillery gun, for details of which see p. 30.

The peace strengths of the batteries are identical with the war strengths in the above table, except in the case of the mountain horse battery, which maintains in peace only 163 combatants and 34 non-combatants, and in that of No. 7 mountain battery, which has only 13 non-combatants. No. 2 heavy battery has only 4 guns horsed in peace.

Engineers.—The Turkestan sapper half-battalion consists of two companies of sappers, with heliograph detachment of 1 officer and 20 rank and file.

A company = 3 officers, 219 combatants.
Half-battalion = 14 „ 480 „

In addition there is a section of non-combatants of 31 rank and file with 36 horses.

Local troops.—There are 12 small bodies of infantry quartered at the following points :—

Aulie-ata (247), Charjui (202), Chimkent (278), Djizak (197), Djulek (123), Karmaktchinsk (123), Katti-kurgan (215), Kazalinsk (312), Khodjent (308), Perovsk (215), Turkestan (214), Ura-tiube (139).

Fortress artillery.—There is one company at Samarkand (224) and one at Tashkent (224).

The strength of all ranks in peace and war is given in the table below :—

	Field Troops.					Local Troops.		Grand Total.	
	Infantry.	Cavalry.	Artillery.	Engineers.	Total.	Infantry.	Artillery.	Men.	Guns.
Peace ...	18,022	3,074	2,345	525	23,966	2,583	448	26,997	64
War ...	25,038	3,074	2,492	525	31,129	2,583	448	34,190	68

About 1,000 horses are required on mobilisation, mainly for the artillery.

OMSK.

The boundaries of the military district of Omsk, which comprises the governments and provinces of Semirechia, Semipalatinsk, Akmolinsk, Tomsk, and Tobolsk, are roughly defined as follows. On the north the Arctic Ocean ; on the west a line running generally due south from Kara Bay to the Saumal Lake, in lat. : 45° N., long. : 68° E. ; on the south, the boundary of the Turkestan military district from the Saumal Lake to the Chinese frontier, at a point nearly 100 miles north of the Karakul Lake, thence the Chinese frontier as far as long. 90° : E. ; from this point the eastern boundary runs to the N.N.W. to the Gulf of Taz.

The head-quarters of the district are at the town of Omsk, on the Irtysh, in the province of Akmolinsk.

ORGANISATION.

The troops quartered within the district consist of (see p. 64).

Field Troops.

Infantry—7 West Siberian frontier battns.
Cavalry—3 regts. Siberian Cossacks, 6 sqns. each.
1 regt. Semirechia Cossacks, 4 sqns.
Artillery—W. Siberian bde., 4 batts., 8 guns each.
1 mountain horse battery, 6 guns.
Engineers—1 West Siberian Sapper Company.

Reserve Troops.

Infantry—4 reserve infantry cadre battalions.
Cavalry—6 regts. Siberian Cossacks, 6 sqns. each.
2 regts. Semirechia Cossacks, 4 sqns. each.

Local Troops.

Infantry—35 local detachments.

Strength.

Infantry.—The infantry consists of 7 West Siberian frontier battalions, numbered from 1 to 8 (but the 2nd battalion is detached to Vladivostok in the Pri-amur district, see p. 18), each of 4 companies.

Company	Peace 3 officers,	166 combatants.
	War 4 "	240 "
Battalion	Peace 17 officers,	668 combatants.
	War 21 "	960 "

In addition the battalion has a non-combatant section of 3 officials, 58 rank and file, and 35 horses.

Cavalry.—The cavalry consists of the 1st, 2nd, and 3rd regiments of Siberian Cossacks, each of 6 squadrons, and of the 1st Semirechia Cossack regiment of 4 squadrons. The peace and war strength of combatants may be stated roughly as—

Squadron	= 3 officers,	148 men,	150 horses.
Siberian regt.	= 21 "	880 "	902 "
Semirechia regt.	= 15 "	600 "	619 "

Each regiment has a non-combatant section of—Siberian regiment, 3 officials, 111 rank and file, and 154 horses; Semirechia regiment, 4 officials, 55 rank and file, and 84 horses.

Artillery.—The West Siberian brigade consists of 4 batteries of 8 guns each; Nos. 1, 2, and 4 are light field batteries,* No. 3 is a mountain battery. In addition, there is the West Siberian mountain horse

---

* Nos. 1 and 2 batteries, though denominated as, and having the establishment of personnel for, light field batteries, are armed with the horse artillery gun, for details of which see p 30.

battery. The peace and war establishments of the field and mountain batteries are practically the same as those given for Nos. 3 to 6 and No. 7 batteries in Turkestan on p. 10.

The mountain horse battery, though it has the same war effective as the Turkestan battery, has a peace establishment of only 63 of all ranks, with 45 horses, and 2 guns.

Depôts of 38 men each are maintained for the light batteries.

Engineers.—The West Siberian Sapper Company* consists of—

In peace,	7 officers,	144 combatants,	10 non-combatants.
In war,	7 „	259 „	13 „

Reserve infantry consists of the Tobolsk, Tomsk, Omsk, and Semipalatinsk reserve cadre battalions.

The strengths of these battalions in peace-time are respectively: 565 750, 1,024, and 557 of all ranks, each battalion being divided into 5 companies.

In war these cadre battalions expand as follows: the Tobolsk and Tomsk battalions each form 2, the Omsk forms 3, independent reserve battalions, and the Semipalatinsk battalion forms a reserve field regiment of 4 battalions, and 1 independent reserve battalion, making 12 battalions in all, each of 4 companies.

Company	= 3 officers,	240 combatants.
Independent battn.	= 16 „	960 „
Regiment	= 63 „	3,835 „

There is a non-combatant section of 2 officials and 26 rank and file for the independent battalion, and a company of 7 officials, 159 rank and file, and 158 horses for the regiment.

Reserve cavalry consists of 4 Cossack regiments of the 2nd line, viz., 4th, 5th, and 6th regiments of Siberian Cossacks, each of 6 squadrons, and the 2nd Semirechia regiment of 4 squadrons—and of 4 Cossack

* The company comprises a small telegraph and heliograph detachment, which on mobilization requires 62 additional horses.

regiments of the 3rd line, of similar composition to the foregoing, viz., 7th, 8th, 9th Siberian, and 3rd Semirechian regiments. The strength of these units is identical with that given for the Cossack troops on p. 13.

NOTE.—The length of service in the field class for Cossack troops is 12 years, divided into three equal periods, known as 1st, 2nd, and 3rd lines. Men in the 1st line constitute the personnel of the regiments, batteries, &c., serving in peace. Men of the 2nd and 3rd lines are on furlough during peace, but on mobilization may be called up to form the regiments and batteries of the 2nd and 3rd lines, small cadres for which are attached to the units of the 1st line in peace. Cossacks of the second line are bound to keep their horse and equipment ready for service, those of the 3rd line maintain their equipment only.

The places of assembly of the Cossack regiments of the second and third lines are—

Siberian regiments, Nos. 4 and 7	Akmolinsk. Kokchetavsk. Présnovsk.
Siberian regiments, Nos. 5 and 8	Cherlakovsk. Omsk. Petropavlovsk.
Siberian regiments, Nos. 6 and 9	Charyshsk. Pavlodarsk. Semipalatinsk. Ust-Kamenogorsk. Zaisansk.
Semirechia regiments, Nos. 2 and 3	Almatinsk. Koksuisk. Kopal. Sergiopol.

Local infantry are maintained as follows:—In the government of Tobolsk 10 detachments, amounting to 1,607 of all ranks; in Tomsk 8, amounting to 1,635; in Akmolinsk 4, amounting to 605; in Semipalatinsk 5, amounting to 1003*; and in Semirechia 8, amounting to 1,764; total, 6,614.

* In peace 662 only.

The strength of the troops in the Omsk Military district is as follows :—

	Field Troops.					Reserve.		Local Infantry.	Grand Total.	
	Infantry.	Cavalry.	Artillery.	Engineers.	Total.	Infantry.	Cavalry.		Men.	Guns.
Peace	5,229	3,716	962	159	10,066	2,896	—	6,273	19,235	34
War...	7,245	3,716	1,198	279	12,438	11,928	7,432	6,641	38,412	38

About 5,000 horses would be required on mobilization, a large proportion of which would be required for the Cossack regiments of the 3rd line.

IRKUTSK.

The Irkutsk military district, comprising the governments of Yenissei, Irkutsk, and Yakutsk, is bounded on the north by the Glacial Ocean; on the west by the eastern boundary of the Omsk military district, see p. 12; on the south by the Russo-Chinese frontier from long. 90° E., up to the vicinity of Lake Baikal; and thence on the south and east by an irregular line along Lake Baikal, and the crests of the Yablonnoi and Stanovoi ranges. The head-quarters of the district are at Irkutsk.

Organisation.

The troops quartered in the district consist of (*see* p. 65).

Infantry—2 reserve cadre battalions.
9 local detachments.
Cavalry—2 squadrons of Cossacks.

STRENGTH.

Infantry.—The two reserve cadre battalions are stationed at Krasnoyarsk, and Irkutsk, from which places they take their names.

The former has a peace effective of 956, the latter of 1,166 of all ranks, each being divided into 5 companies.

On mobilisation the Irkutsk cadre battalion expands and forms a reserve regiment of 4 battalions, and an independent reserve battalion ; the Krasnoyarsk cadre battalion forms a reserve regiment of 2 battalions, and an independent reserve battalion ; in all these cases the battalion is of 4 companies, the strength of a company being 3 officers and 240 combatants. The strength of the various units is as below—

	Officers.	Combatants.	Non-combatants.	Total Rank and File.	Horses.
Independent battalion	18	958	26	984	8
2 battalion regiment ...	39	1,920	70	1,990	108
4 battalion regiment ...	70	3,835	159	3,994	159

Local detachments are maintained at the following places, Achinsk (176), Alexandrovsk (225), Balagansk (37), Kansk (189), Kirensk (96), Minusinsk (187), Nijne-Udinsk (91), Yakutsk (179), Yenissei (112) ; total, 1,292 all ranks.

Cavalry.—Two squadrons of Cossacks are maintained, the one at Irkutsk, the other at Krasnoyarsk : the former has a strength of 143, the latter of 99 of all ranks.

The strength of the troops in the district is as under :—

	Infantry.		Cavalry.	Grand Total.	
	Reserve Troops.	Local Troops.	Cossacks.	Men.	Guns.
Peace	2,122	1,292	242	3,656	—
War	8,097	1,292	242	9,631	—

Some 300 horses will be required on mobilisation.

PRI-AMUR.

The Pri-amur military district, which includes the provinces of Primorsk, Trans-baikal, South Ussuria, and the island of Saghalien, is bounded on the north and west by the Glacial Ocean, and by the southern and eastern boundary line of the Irkutsk military district; on the south by the Russo-Chinese frontier; and on the east by the various inlying seas of the Northern Pacific Ocean. The headquarters of the military district are at Khabarovka.

Organisation.

The troops quartered in the district are (see p. 66)—

Field Troops.

Infantry—2 E. Siberian rifle bdes., 5 battns. each.
5 East Siberian frontier battalions.
1 West " " "
2 Cossack battalions.
2 Cossack half-battalions.

Cavalry—2 squadrons Ussurian horse.
2 Cossack regiments, 6 squadrons each.

Artillery—E. Siberian bde., 4 batts., 8 guns each.
2 Cossack horse batts., 6 guns each.

Engineers—East Siberian sapper company.

Reserve Troops.

Infantry—1 infantry reserve cadre battalion.
4 battalions Cossack infantry.
Cavalry—2 Cossack regiments of 6 squadrons each.
Artillery—1 Cossack horse battery.

Local Troops.

Infantry—11 local detachments.
Artillery—3 fortress companies.

STRENGTH.

Infantry.—The East Siberian rifles are organised in two brigades, each of five battalions (the battalions being numbered from 1 to 10) of 4 companies. The East Siberian frontier battalions (Nos. 1 to 5), and the 2nd West Siberian frontier battalion, are also each of 4 companies. Nearly all these troops are maintained on the war footing of 1,036 all ranks.

The only exception is the 2nd West Siberian battalion, which in peace has a slightly smaller effective of 833 all ranks.

A company = 4 officers, 240 combatants.
A battalion = 21 " 960 "

In addition the battalion has a non-combatant section of 4 officials, 58 non-combatants, and 35 to 43 horses.

The Cossack infantry consists of 2 Trans-baikal battalions, each of 5 companies, 1 Amur half-battalion, and one Ussurian half-battalion ; the two latter consist of 3 companies each in war.

One company only in each of the half battalions is kept with the colours in peace, the others being on furlough.

A company = 4 officers, 180 combatants.
A half-battalion = 12 " 550 "
A battalion = 22 " 910 "

The half-battalion has a non-combatant section of 3 officials, 33 non-combatants, and 35 horses; a battalion one of 2, 38, and 27 respectively.

Cavalry.—The cavalry consists of 2 squadrons Ussurian horse, 1 Trans-baikal Cossack regiment, and 1 Amur Cossack regiment, each of 6 squadrons.

In peace the Amur Cossack regiment consists of only 2 squadrons.

A squadron= 3 officers, 148 combatants, 151 horses.
A regiment=21 „ 890 „ 914 „

The regiment has in addition a non-combatant section of 4 officials, 58 rank and file, with 115 horses.

Artillery.—The East Siberian brigade consists of 4 batteries, of which Nos. 1 and 2 are light field, Nos. 3 and 4 mountain batteries. There are also the 2 Trans-baikal Cossack horse batteries and a mobile artillery half park. The strength of these units is as below—

Battery.	Officers.		Com-batants.		Non-com-batants.		Horses.		Guns.	
	Peace.	War.	Peace.	War.	Peace.	War.	Peace.	War.	Peace.	War.
Light ...	6	6	208	208	23	23	58	181	4	8
Mountain ...	6	6	182	233	13	67	97	206	8	8
Cossack ..	6	5	133	194	15	28	120	265	4	6

In peace a light battery maintains a cadre of 71 rank and file, 40 horses, and 4 mountain guns, to enable it to act as mountain artillery if required.

In war, depôts are maintained of 38 rank and file for each light battery, and of 44 rank and file and 16 horses for each Cossack battery.

Engineers.—The East Siberian sapper company has a strength of 6 officers, 238 combatants, and 16 non-combatants, with 16 horses in both peace and war.

Reserve infantry consists of the Strétinsk reserve cadre battalion, and of 4 battalions of Trans-baikal Cossack infantry* (viz., 2 regiments of the second and 2 of the 3rd line).

In peace the Stretinsk battalion is of 5 companies, with a total strength of 555 of all ranks.

In war the Strétinsk battalion, on mobilisation, expands into one reserve regiment of 4 battalions, and one independent reserve battalion, each battalion being of 4 companies.

Company	= 3 officers,	240 combatants.	
Independent battn.	= 16 „	960	„
Regiment	= 63 „	3,835	„

In addition there are non-combatants; a section of 2 officials and 26 rank and file for the independent battalion, and a company of 7 officials, 159 rank and file, and 158 horses for the regiment.

The Cossack infantry battalions of the 2nd and 3rd lines, are of precisely similar strength to those of the 1st line given on p. 19.

Reserve cavalry is formed by the Cossacks of the 2nd and 3rd lines* (for explanation of which see p. 15), and consists of—

2 Trans-baikal Cossack regts. of 6 sqdns. each.

The strength of these units is the same as that given for the Cossacks of the 1st line on p. 20.

Reserve artillery consists of one Trans-baikal Cossack horse battery* of the same strength as that given for a Cossack battery in the table on p. 20.

Local troops.—There are the following detachments of infantry:—

In Trans-baikal province; Chita (184), Nerchinsk (113), Verkhne-udinsk (133).

---

* The three recruiting districts for these formations in Trans-baikal are Troitskosavsk, Aksha, and Nertchinsk.

In Primorsk province; De Castries Bay (127), Nikolaievsk (228), Olga Bay (127), Suchan (111).

In Saghalien; Alexandrovsk (341), Dué (346), Korsakovsk (235), Tymov (341).

Fortress artillery.—There are 2 companies at Vladivostok (each 339) and 1 at Nikolaievsk (104).

The strength of all ranks on the peace and war footings is given below:—

	Field Troops.					Reserves.			Local Troops.		Grand Total.	
	Infantry.	Cavalry.	Artillery.	Engineers.	Total.	Infantry.	Cavalry.	Artillery.	Infantry.	Artillery.	Men.	Guns.
Peace	18,729	1,768	1,326	260	22,083	555	—	—	2,286	782	25,706	40
War ...	19,716	2,287	1,704	260	23,967	8,596	1,946	271	2,286	782	37,848	50

About 3,000 horses would be required on mobilisation, half of which are wanted for the Cossacks of the 3rd line.

CHAPTER II.

UNIFORM, EQUIPMENT, &c.

N.B.—During the hot weather of summer the regular troops wear a white linen blouse with coloured cloth shoulder straps, the same as those on the tunic described further on, and the forage cap is encased in a white linen cover, which completely conceals the cap-band. In Turkestan and Transcaspia leather breeches, dyed a reddish colour, are worn in the field and at manœuvres.

INFANTRY.*

Uniform.—Tunic of dark-green cloth, double-breasted, fastening with hooks, with coloured shoulder straps and collar patches. Trousers dark green without stripe. Forage cap dark green with coloured band. Great coat of grey homespun, with coloured shoulder straps and collar patches. Long knee boots into which the ends of the trousers are tucked.

The various units are distinguished by the colour and insignia of the shoulder straps, collar patches, and cap-bands, as shown in the following table.

---

* See Plate I at the end of the book.

	Unit.	Shoulder-strap.		Collar-patch on		Cap-band.	
		Colour.	In-signia.	Tunic.	Great-coat.	Colour.	In-signia.
Rifles	Transcaspian	crimson	No. of battn. and *3K*	none ...	green ...	green, crimson piping	No. of battn. and **3K**
	Turkestan ...	"	No. of battn. and *III*	"	"	"	No. of battn. and **T**
	East Siberian	"	No. of battn. and *BC*	"	"	"	No. of battn. and **BC**
Frontier battalions	Turkestan ...	light blue	No. of battn. and *III*	scarlet	scarlet	scarlet	No. of battn. and **T**
	West Siberian	"	No. of battn. and *3C*	"	"	"	No. of battn. and **3C**
	East Siberian	"	No. of battn. and *BC*	"	"	"	No of battn. and **BC**
Cossack Infantry	Transbaikal	yellow	No. of battn. and *3*	none ...	yellow	yellow	cockade.
	Amur ...	green, yellow piping	No. of battn. and *A*	"	green, yellow piping	"	"
	Ussuria ...	"	No. of battn. and *Y*	"	"	"	"
	Reserve troops	scarlet	initial of name of battn.	"	scarlet	scarlet	initial of battn. and **P**
	Local troops	green, scarlet piping	none ...	"	green	green, scarlet piping	letter **M**

Badges of Rank.—N.C.O. are distinguished by stripes of yellow or white braid across the shoulder strap, 1 for lance corporal, 2 for corporal, 3 for sergeant. Sergeant-major, 1 stripe of gold or silver lace across shoulder strap, and lace on cuffs. Volunteers have a cord of orange, black, and white as edging to the shoulder strap. Re-engaged men a stripe of silver lace on left arm.

Officers have their badges of rank on the shoulder strap. The ground of the shoulder-strap is of the same coloured cloth as that of the men of the unit to which the officer belongs; but it is ornamented with longitudinal stripes of gold or silver lace, between which the coloured cloth shows. For general officers the shoulder strap is of plain gold or silver lace, with no cloth stripe showing; for field officers two longitudinal cloth stripes: for company officers one. The different ranks in each of these grades is shown by the stars on the shoulder-straps, as in the table below:—

Badge.	General Officers.	Field Officers.	Company Officers.
No Star	General	Colonel	Captain
4 Stars	..	..	2nd Captain
3 "	Lieut.-General	Lieut.-Col.	Lieutenant
2 "	Major-General	..	Sub.-Lieutenant
1 "	..	..	Ensign

The above badges of rank are the same for all arms of the service.

Armament.—Berdan rifle and bayonet (always carried fixed). Calibre of rifle, ·42 inch; charge, 77 grs.; bullet, 370 grs.; muzzle velocity, 1,444 feet. Rifle sighted to 1,500 paces (1,160 yards); long-range firing up to 1,720 yards.

Officers and sergeant-majors armed with sword and revolver; the latter Smith and Wesson six-chambered, double-action. Calibre, ·42 inch; charge, 23 grs.; bullet, 233½ grs.; muzzle velocity, 656 feet; point-blank range, 150 yards.

Equipment.—A waterproof havresack over the right shoulder, one water-bottle, spare pair of boots, one mess-tin, one-sixth of shelter tent; weight carried, 63¼ lb.

Ammunition.—84 rounds on the person, viz., 60 in two pouches, 24 in havresack; 48 rounds per man in regimental transport. For revolvers, 12 rounds per man on the person.

Entrenching Tools.—80 Linnemann spades and 20 light axes are carried by the men of each company. All rank and file of the train, *in all arms*, carry entrenching tools—half of them spades, half axes.

Supplies.—Carried on the person, biscuit and salt for 2½ days. Battalion transport—biscuit, 1½ days; other stores, 3 to 6 days.

Transport.—A rifle battalion has 8 S.A.A., 1 pharmacy, 1 medical store, 1 battalion and 2 officers' carts, 8 company and 3 battalion wagons and 1 ambulance. Total, 25 vehicles, 43 horses, and 30 rank and file.

This transport is divided into 2 lines; the first, following immediately in rear of the battalion, consists of 4 S.A.A., 1 pharmacy, 1 medical store, 2 officers' carts and 1 ambulance; the second, in rear of the whole column, of. 4 S.A.A. and 1 battalion carts, 8 company and 3 regimental wagons, with 4 spare horses.

The transport of a frontier battalion is governed by special instructions, but it differs probably very little from the foregoing.

All vehicles are painted dark green, with the name of the unit to which they belong marked on the near side.

Cavalry.

N.B. The Cossacks in Turkestan, and probably also in other parts of Asiatic Russia, wear during the hot

* See Plate II at the end of the book.

weather a frock made of grey camel's hair cloth, with shoulder straps of the regulation pattern.

Uniform.—The Kuban Cossacks (in Transcaspia) wear the Circassian costume; a long dark brown coat, having cartridge recesses on the breast, with scarlet shoulder straps, and under garment (or waistcoat) of scarlet, and dark trousers—forage cap of the usual pattern with red piping. The initial letter of the name of the regiment is borne on the shoulder strap, *e.g.*, *K* for Kavkaz regiment.

The other Cossacks in Asiatic Russia wear an ordinary single-breasted tunic* and striped pantaloons, both of the same coloured cloth. The particulars of the various Cossack uniforms are given in the table below.

	Orenburg.	Ural.	Astrakhan.	Siberian.	Semirechian.	Irkutsk and Krasnoyarsk.	Ussurian and Amur.	Transbaikal.
Uniform ...	green	blue	blue	green	green	green	green	green
Cap-band ...	blue, yellow piping	crimson piping	yellow piping	scarlet	crimson	yellow	green, yellow piping	yellow
Shoulder straps — Colour	blue, yellow piping	crimson	yellow	scarlet	crimson	yellow	green, yellow piping	yellow
Shoulder straps — Insignia	No. of regt.	No. of regt.	No. of regt.	*C*	No. of regt. and *C*	initial of district.	initial of district.	No. of regt. and *3*
Trouser stripes	yellow	crimson	yellow	scarlet	crimson	yellow	yellow	yellow

Standards and guidons.—Each Cossack regiment has a standard of the same colour as the body of the regimental shoulder strap. In the regiments of the Orenburg, Siberian, Semirechian, and Transbaikal

* The tunic of the Ural Cossacks is double-breasted.

districts the standard has two diagonal white stripes, in order to distinguish these regiments from those of other districts having standards of the same colour. The standards of the Amur regiments have similar diagonal stripes, but of yellow. In the centre of the standard the number or initial letter of the name of the regiment is marked in yellow, if the body ground is red, crimson, or blue; in red, if yellow or dark green.

Each squadron has a burgee-shaped guidon, the upper half of which is of the same colour as the body ground of the regimental standard; in the case of those regiments in which the regimental standard is marked by diagonal stripes, a bar of similar colour runs through the centre of the upper half of the guidon. The lower half of the guidon indicates the squadron, the following sequence of colours being observed: 1st squadron scarlet, 2nd blue, 3rd white, 4th dark-green, 5th yellow, 6th cinnamon brown.

Armament.—All Cossacks are armed with the Berdan cavalry rifle, same as that in use in infantry, but slightly shorter, carried slung over left shoulder; sighted up to 1,200 paces (930 yards); long-range firing up to 1,500 paces (1,160 yards). Officers, sergeant-majors, and trumpeters armed with sword and revolver, the latter of same pattern as in the Infantry.

In the Ural and Astrakhan Cossacks the front rank is armed with the lance, and both ranks are so armed in the Transbaikal, Amur, Ussuria, Irkutsk, and Krasnoyarsk Cossacks. The other Asiatic Cossacks have no lances; but all Cossacks in Asia are armed with the sword, which is 3 feet 4 inches long, without a guard, worn slung over the right shoulder.

Equipment.—The bridle is a single bridoon, the saddle is of the high-peaked Cossack pattern, with two girths, surcingle, and breastplate, having two wallets in front, and a valise in rear. The cornsack, greatcoat, and $\frac{1}{6}$ of shelter tent are carried in front; blankets, mess-tin, and hay net in rear.

Every Cossack carries a whip, and consequently no spurs are worn.

The average weight carried by the horse is 18 to 20 stone.

Ammunition.—Rifles: 36 rounds on the person, in two pouches; 36 rounds per man in regimental transport. Revolvers: 12 rounds on the person.

Entrenching Tools, &c.—20 light shovels, 20 axes per squadron, on the saddles; 4 large spades, 4 light axes per squadron, in regimental transport; 6 pairs of bladders per squadron in regimental transport; 1 set of tools for construction of bridges, ferries, &c., per squadron; reserve of gun-cotton for the whole regiment in regimental transport.

Supplies.—Carried on the saddle, 1½ days' biscuit, 2 days' salt, and other supplies. Carried in the regimental transport 2½ days' biscuit, other stores 2 days, and 1 day's preserved provisions. Carried on the saddle, 13 lb. oats, 20 lb. hay.*

Transport.—Regimental transport is divided into two lines as in the infantry.

1st line; 6 S.A.A., 2 pharmacy and medical carts, 2 ambulances, 6 squadron wagons; 2nd line, 14 regimental wagons, 1 veterinary, and 1 headquarter's carts. Total, 32 vehicles, 64 horses, 37 rank and file. There are also 33 led horses.

The above is for a 6 squadron regiment: in the case of 4 squadron regiment, the numbers are proportionately reduced.

Artillery.†

(a) *Field and Mountain Artillery.*

Uniform.—Very similar to that for infantry, but no patches on tunic collar, which has scarlet piping on both

---

* *I.e.* 1¼ days' corn and 2 days' hay if on short rations, or 1 day's corn and 1¼ days' hay on full rations.

† See Plate III at the end of the book.

upper and lower edges; the great-coat collar has black patches with scarlet piping. Shoulder straps of scarlet with certain insignia as given below; cap and cap-bands black with scarlet piping, with the number of the battery in yellow.

The insignia on the shoulder straps are as follows: Batteries in Transcaspia the number of the brigade to which they belong, see p. 7, those of the Turkestan brigade the letter *Т*; of the West Siberian brigade the letters *ЗС*; of the East Siberian brigade the letters *ВС*

Armament and matériel.—On the war footing the composition of batteries is as follows:—Heavy battery, 8 guns and 16 ammunition wagons; light battery 8 guns, 12 ammunition wagons; mountain battery, 8 guns 128 ammunition boxes; each battery has a spare gun carriage. Particulars of guns, including the horse artillery weapon, are given below:—

N.B.—The 3rd and 4th batteries of the Turkestan brigade, and the 1st and 2nd batteries of the West Siberian brigade, are armed with the horse artillery gun, but in all other respects they are actually, as they are denominated, light field batteries.

Nature of Battery.	Weight behind Team.	Gun.		Weight of—			Muzzle Velocity.	Extreme Range.
		Calibre.	Weight.	Common Shell.	Service Charge.	Bursting Charge.		
	cwt.	ins.	cwt.	lb.	lb.	oz.	f.s.	yards.
Heavy ...	50¼	4·2	12⅓	27⅓	4 1/16	14½	1,225	5,250
Light ...	45¼	3·42	9	15⅛	3	7	1,450	7,000
Mountain ...	...	2·5	2	8¼	13⅓ oz.	4¼	932	3,500 (?)
Horse ...	31½	3·42	7	15⅛	3 lb.	7	1,350	7,000

The number of rounds carried per battery is—

Heavy	864
Light	1,200
Mountain	720
Horse	780
Mountain horse....	540

All ranks are armed with a sabre and revolver, for which each man carries 12 rounds. Gunners carry the knapsack, water bottle, mess tin, and part of tent, as in the infantry. Mounted men as in the cavalry.

Entrenching Tools.—Carried with the battery. Field battery: 32 spades, 24 axes, 4 mattocks, 4 saws, 2 crowbars: Mountain battery; 61 spades, 16 axes, 16 mattocks, 16 picks, 4 saws, 4 crowbars. Nil in regimental train.

Supplies.—Field battery: carried on the person, or with kit, biscuit and salt for 3 days; in battery wagons 1 day's biscuit, other stores 2 to 6 days. Mountain battery: on the person as above; in battery train, biscuit 2 days, groats 6 days, other stores 14 days, and 1 day's preserved provisions. Carried on the saddle 3 days' oats. In the battery train: Field battery, 1½ days' oats for riding and draught horses; Mountain battery, 2 days' oats for riding (7) and draught horses (118), 3 days' oats for transport horses (54); led and spare horses carry their own supplies.

Transport.—Field battery: (*a*) Artillery train 1 four-horsed wagon, 4 pair-horsed wagons; (*b*) Supply train, 3 pair-horsed wagons. Total train, 8 vehicles, 21 horses, 10 rank and file. Mountain battery: pack train of 54 pack, 6 spare horses, and 52 rank and file.

(*b*) Horse Artillery.

The horse artillery in Asiatic Russia consists entirely of Cossack horse batteries.

Uniform.—As for Cossack cavalry, except that the shoulder strap bears the number of the battery instead of that of the regiment, and the pantaloons are without stripes. In the case of the 4th Kuban battery in Transcaspia the letter K is borne on the shoulder strap.

Armament and matériel.—The battery consists of 6 guns, 12 ammunition wagons, and 1 spare carriage. For nature of gun and rounds carried, see under field artillery. All ranks armed with sabre and revolver, for which ammunition is carried as in field artillery.

Entrenching Tools.—32 spades, 18 axes, 4 mattocks, 4 picks, 4 saws, 2 crowbars, carried with the battery.

Supplies.—Carried on the saddle, 1½ days' biscuit, 2 days' salt, and other supplies. Carried in battery train, 2½ days' biscuit, other stores 2 to 4 days, and 1 day's preserved provisions. Oats for riding horses; carried on the saddle as in the cavalry; in regimental train, 1½ days' supply for draught horses.

Transport.—(*a*) Artillery Train; 1 four-horsed wagon, 4 pair-horsed wagons; (*b*) Supply Train; 1 pharmacy cart, 1 ambulance, 4 pair-horsed wagons. Total, 11 vehicles, 28 horses, 14 men.

(*c*) Mountain Horse Artillery.

Uniform.—Tunic dark green with scarlet shoulder straps, on which are the letters *Кон. Гор.*,* with *Т* for the Turkestan, and *ЗС* for the West Siberian battery. Pantaloons of French grey. Cap dark green, with dark-green band and scarlet piping. In other respects as for field artillery.

Armament and matériel.—These batteries consist of 6 guns, 12 ammunition wagons, 1 spare carriage, and are armed with the mountain gun, see p. 30. Armament of personnel as for horse artillery.

* See p. 57.

Entrenching Tools.—As for horse artillery.

Supplies.—As for mountain artillery ; but two days' oats are carried for 108 riding, and 68 battery horses, and 3 days' oats for 47 pack horses of the battery train.

Transport.—The battery has a pack train of 14 horses with artillery stores, 47 horses with supplies, and 5 spare horses. Total, 66 horses, with 49 rank and file.

(*d*) FORTRESS ARTILLERY.

Uniform.—As for field artillery, but the shoulder strap bears the initial letter of the locality to which the company belongs.

Armament.—The men are armed with Berdan rifle (infantry pattern) and revolvers.

Matériel.—The normal armament of coast batteries is made up of one-half 9″ guns, the other half consisting of 14″, 11″, 8″, and 6″ guns ; 9″ mortars are also employed. Land fortresses, and land fronts of coast fortresses, have a normal armament of 70% of short 24-prs., and 30 % of 8″ guns and long 24-prs. ; rifled mortars in the proportion of one-tenth the number of rifled guns.

The principal particulars of the above guns are given in the table below :—

Nature of Ordnance.	Gun.			Weight of			Muzzle Velocity.	Extreme Range.
	Length.	Weight.	Calibre.	Shell.	Service Charge.	Bursting Charge.		
Sea Fronts.	feet.	tons	ins.	lb.	lb.	lb.	f.s.	yds.
14″ gun	26¼	57½	14	1489½	198½	46½	1,300	8,150
11″ ,, ...	20	28¼	11	550¾	115½	25¼	1,400	7,000
9″ ,, ...	16½	15	9	278	64½	11	1,500	7,000
8″ ,, ...	14½	9	8	165¼	28½	11¼	1,330	7,000
6″ ,, ...	11	cwt. 61	6	83½	19	3½	1,464	3,500
9″ mortar ...	9	tons. 5½	9	278	29	11	951	7,000
Land Fronts.								
8″ light gun ...	11	5¾	8	196	17	7¾	995	3,500
24-pr. long gun...	10¾	cwt. 44	6	64	6¼	2¼	1,063	5,800
24-pr. short gun	7¼	31	6	64	3½	2¼	727	4,200

ENGINEERS.

Uniform.—Dark green tunic and collar, the latter with scarlet piping, no collar patch, shoulder straps scarlet with insignia as below. Great-coat grey, with scarlet piping on collar and dark green collar patch. Cap and cap-band dark green with scarlet piping, and insignia as below. Buttons of white metal. In other respects as for infantry.

	Trans-caspian.	Turkestan.	West Siberian.	East Siberian.
Shoulder-straps	*З.К.*	*Ш.*	*З.С.*	*В.С.*
Cap-bands	З.К.С.	Т.С.	З.С.С.	В.С.С.

Armament and equipment.—Armament as for infantry, equipment as for field artillery.

Ammunition.—84 rounds per rifle carried by the men; 23 rounds in company transport. Revolver ammunition; 12 rounds carried by the men so armed.

Entrenching Tools.—Per company: Carried by the men of each company, 100 spades, 70 axes, 20 mattocks, 10 picks, 4 saws; in company transport, 40 spades, 24 light, 16 heavy axes, 18 picks, mattocks, &c., 2 saws, 2 crow-bars: a variety of tools for bridging purposes, and gun-cotton and powder for demolitions.

Supplies.—Carried by the men, biscuit and salt for 2½ days; in company transport 5½ days' biscuit and salt other stores 8 days.

Transport.—Turkestan sapper half battalion: 2 S.A.A., 1 office, 2 supply, 1 medical wagons, and 1 ambulance 4 tool wagons. Total, 11 vehicles, 47 horses, and 13 rank and file. Sapper companies, 5 or 6 vehicles, 15 to 16 horses, and 6 to 14 rank and file.

CHAPTER III.

TACTICS, &c.

MARCHES.

Rate of Marching.—Infantry, 116 to 120 paces (of 28 inches) per minute, $2\frac{2}{3}$ miles per hour, $13\frac{1}{3}$ to $16\frac{2}{3}$ miles per day (7 to 9 hours); 66 miles per week (5 days' marching, 2 days' halt). Field artillery, about 3 miles an hour. Cavalry and horse artillery walk $3\frac{1}{3}$ miles per hour, trot $6\frac{2}{3}$ miles per hour, trot and walk alternately $4\frac{2}{3}$ miles per hour. Average day's march 20 to 26 miles in $5\frac{1}{2}$ to 8 hours.

Under favourable conditions, infantry are considered capable of marching $32\frac{1}{2}$, cavalry and horse artillery 47 miles per day.

Breadth of front.—According to circumstances, infantry in fours, column of half sections (front of 12 men), or column of sections; artillery column of route, or column of sections; cavalry in threes or sixes.

Depth of formation.—The following are the regulation distances:—

Between	companies	8 yards.
„	battalions or squadrons	40 „
„	battery and battalion, or squadron	40 „

The road space occupied by the various units is as below.

Infantry in fours—

Company	62 yards.
Battalion	270 „

Artillery in column of route—

Light field battery with 1st line train	530 yards.
Heavy „ „ „	620 „
Horse artillery „ „	580 „

Cavalry—	in threes.	in sixes.
Squadron	125 yards.	62 yards.
Cossack regiment (with train)	1,033 „	660 „

Trains :—

The first échelon* of the train marches immediately in rear of the unit to which it belongs.

The second échelon follows in rear of the whole column at ¼ mile to a half a day's march distant.

Advanced and Rear-Guards, &c.—The strength of the advanced guard is one-sixth to one-fourth that of the main body. For a brigade of four battalions it precedes the main body by ¾ to 1¼ miles ; for a battalion about 600 yards. The advanced guard of the main body in turn detaches a van-guard, which again detaches its covering body, with patrols. When the advanced guard is at some distance from the main body, the latter detaches a small covering body and flanking detachments, in case of the advanced guard being overpowered.

Rear-guards, in case of retreat, are laid down at one-fourth to one-third of the main body.

In case of flank marches the flanking detachment should be one-third of the main body.

---

* *Vide* pp. 26, 29.

Bivouacks.

Infantry battalions bivouack generally in column of companies, or in double column of half companies, with an interval of 15 yards between companies, in which the arms are piled.

Cavalry bivouack generally on a front of 1 squadron, the regiment being in column of squadrons, 20 yards between picket lines.

Artillery on a front of a battery at half interval (9 yards), the guns limbered up, horses picketed 80 yards in rear of the guns and ammunition wagons.

The accompanying plates give the most usual form of the bivouacks.

Guards are furnished by the troops in bivouacks as follows: the advanced guard 150 yards to the front, the bivouack (or quarter) guard 8 yards to the front, and the rear-guard 20 yards to the rear. The advanced or rear-guards throw out a chain of sentries to a distance of 60 to 80 yards, to prevent the approach of unauthorised persons, &c. The strength of the force on duty is usually one-fortieth the main body.

Outposts.

Cavalry is usually employed except within a march of the enemy; when in contact with the enemy infantry is used, cavalry orderlies being attached to carry messages, &c.; in intermediate cases both arms are utilised, artillery being detailed according to circumstances.

Outposts, whether of infantry or cavalry, consist (1) of the piquets (*pósty*) furnishing the line of sentries; (2) of the supports (*zastávy*); and (3) of the reserve (*glávny karaúl*). As far as practicable the principle that the command should be exercised in depth rather than in breadth is observed, each company furnishing

Fig I.

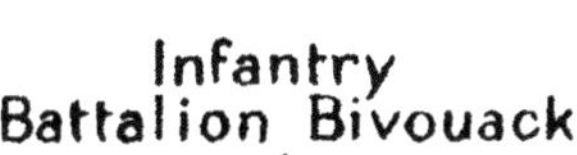

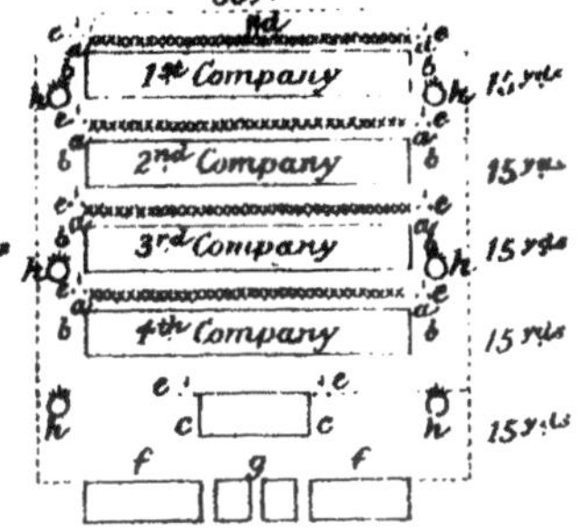

a. a. Arms Piled

b. b. Men in field tents

c. c. Band

d. Drums & Colour

e. Orderlies

f. Subaltern Officers

g. Field Officers

h. Bivouack Fires

Scale 60 yds – 1 Inch.

0 50 100 150 yds

Int: Div: 747a

Fig 2.

CAVALRY

Squadron Bivouack

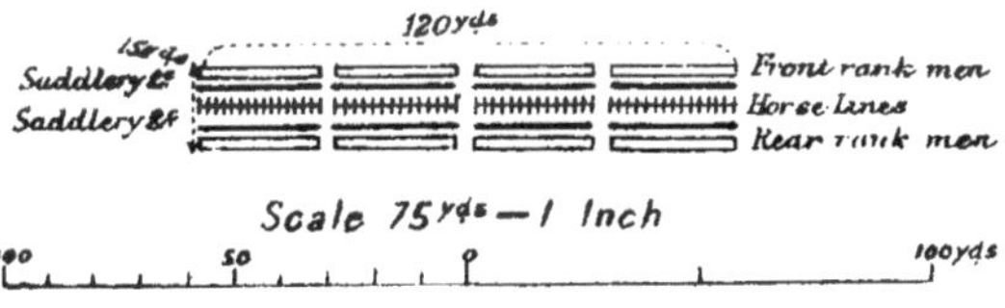

Scale 75 yds — 1 Inch

100 50 0 100 yds

Regimental Bivouack

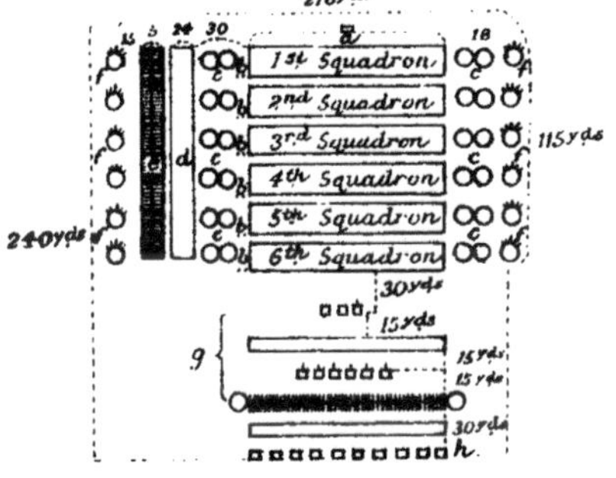

a. Guard
b. Orderlies
c. Forage
d. Officers tents
e. Officers horse lines
f. Bivouack fires
g. Regtl staff, noncombatants &c
h. Kitchens

Scale 150 yds — 1 Inch

100 50 0 100 200 300 yds

Int: Div: 747b

Fig 3.

Bivouack of Field Battery

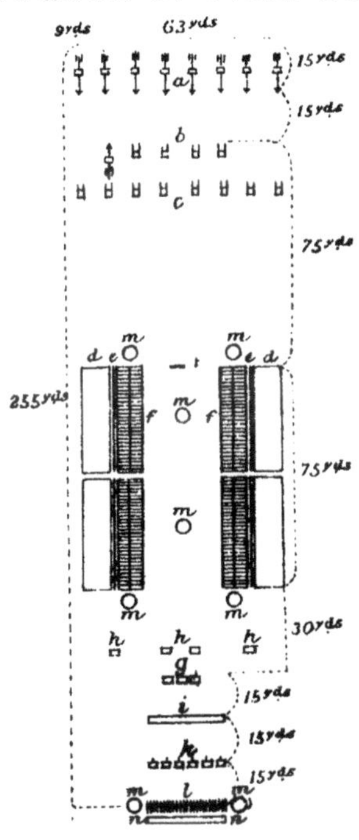

a. Guns limbered up
b. 1st Line of ammunition wagons
c. 2nd ——— do ——— do ———
d. Gunners and Drivers.
e. Harness &c.
f. Battery horse lines
g. Commanding Officer's, Captain's tents, and pay chest with Sentry.
h. Officers tents.
i. Non Combatants.
k. Train.
l. Train horses.
m. Forage.
n. Train drivers.

Scale 75yds – 1 Inch

100 50 0 100yds

Int. Div: 747c

piquets, supports, and reserve. Taking the section of the line of outposts furnished by a company or squadron,* the former would furnish 10 to 15, the latter 8 to 12 piquets, each of 3 to 8 men, according to their position. The piquets furnish one sentry each, posted 8 to 12 yards in close country, 40 yards in open country, in advance of the piquet, if of infantry; 15 to 25 yards and 120 yards respectively, if of cavalry. A man in waiting is placed as support to the sentry half way between him and the piquet. On an average the piquets are 80 to 230 yards apart, if of infantry, and placed in view of one another, so as to command the intervening ground; 230 to 450 yards apart, if of cavalry. Assuming 12 piquets to be put out, a company would cover a front of ¾ to 2 miles, a squadron as much as 3 miles.

A company would furnish two supports of 10 to 25 men, a squadron two of 8 to 12 men each, according to circumstances. The infantry supports are placed about 600 yards, cavalry about 1,200 yards, in rear of the line of piquets.

The remainder of the company or squadron forms the reserve; for the former, placed 600 yards, for the latter 1,200 yards, in rear of the supports. It is not essential in every case that there should be a reserve to the line of outposts, the decision is left to the company commander. Patrols are furnished from the reserve.

In special cases, a special reserve (*resérv*)—in addition to the reserve (or *glávny karaúl*)—may be detailed for the whole of the outpost line, at the discretion of the commander of the outposts.

Piquets and the support in rear of them should, as far as possible, be drawn from the same section, the section N.C.O. being with the support. A company

---

* After allowing for casualties, the company may be taken at 192 bayonets, squadron at 128 sabres.

officer, with the sergeant-major, is in command of the reserve, the other company officers being with the supports, and the company commander being in charge of the whole.

The sentries are relieved at least once every two hours, the outposts every 24 hours; the relief takes place just before daybreak. Fires are not allowed except by special permission.

At night outlying piquets (*sekréty*), consisting of three to five or more men, are sometimes pushed forward 200 to 300 yards in advance of the chain of sentries to conceal themselves in convenient positions. They throw out no sentries, but simply listen for the advance or movement of the enemy, and return at daybreak without being relieved. They are mostly used in face of an energetic enemy, in front of fortified positions, and in Asiatic warfare.

A (1) parole (*paról*), (2) countersign (*ótzyv*), and (3) password (*própusk*) are used: (1) is the name of a town, (2) the name of a saint, (3) some military object. They should all begin with the same letter, *e.g.*, Poltava, Peter, powder; (1) is made known only to officers or N.C.O. acting as such (2) to commanders of patrols and examining posts, (3) to all ranks.

The password is the sign by which friends are recognised; thus, when any person approaches a sentry, the latter challenges, "Halt" (or "Who goes there"), "what is the password?" *Stói* (*kto idyót*), *shtó própusk?*

The countersign, in addition to the password, is given by the patrols in reply to the above challenge by the examining post.

The parole is given by persons arriving with orders from superior authority, as a guarantee to the officer to whom the orders are conveyed that they are genuine.

Fig 4.
Fighting Formation of a Battalion
390 yds
195 yds
195 yds
Skirmishers
Company Zone
Company Zone
Battalion Zone
390 yds
Advanced Line
Company Reserves
2nd Co
1st Co
4th Co
3rd Co
Battalion Reserves
Scale 230 yds — 1 Inch.
0
100
200
300
400
500
600 yds

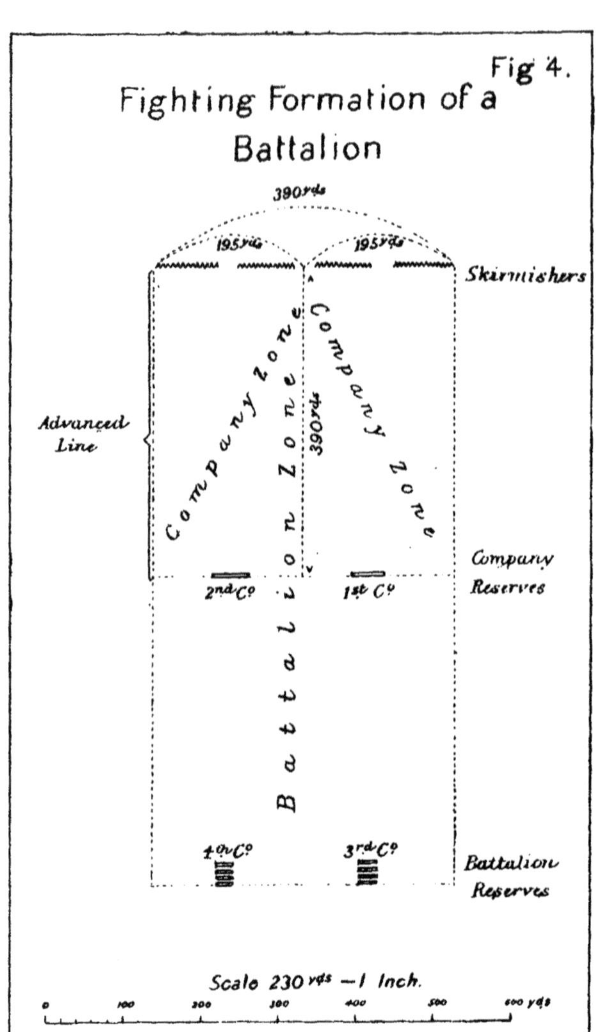

Int: Div: 747d

Tactics.

Infantry.—The company is drawn up in two ranks, and consists of 100 files. Columns of half-companies, sections, and half-sections are formed, either at wheeling distance, or at close interval, which is always 4 yards. The front of the battalion in line is 260 yards; a battalion may also be deployed in line of columns of half-companies, sections, or half-sections, or may form column of companies, half-companies, sections, or half-sections.

In the model attack the leading battalion breaks up into two lines, two companies in 1st and two in 2nd line, at 1,500 or 2,500 yards from the enemy. Each of the companies in 1st line sends out from one section to half a company to form the skirmishing line, the remainder of the company forming the support 400 yards in rear of the skirmishers, the battalion reserve consisting of the two remaining companies, being a similar distance in rear of the supports. Under ordinary circumstances the skirmishers of the company cover a front of 200 yards, thus the normal front of the battalion is 400 yards. The advance takes place from the first zone (which commences 2,500 to 1,500 yards from the enemy) to the second (beginning at 800 to 600 yards) without halts, but before entering this latter the skirmishers are brought up to such a strength as to require no further reinforcements while traversing the second zone.

The advance through the second zone is made by rushes either of the whole line or by alternate portions, the length of the rushes not being more than 80 yards. The supports close up to not more than 150 yards from the skirmishers, opening out if necessary.

The third zone commences at about 250 yards from the enemy, the advance being made by the skirmishers reinforced by the supports, with the reserves just in rear. When within 40 yards of the enemy the charge is made by the skirmishers and reserve combined if necessary. Bayonets are always carried fixed.

Firing at extreme ranges is only carried out under exceptionally favourable circumstances, 600 yards being the extreme limit for individual firing. Volleys may be employed at all ranges, and must be employed in close formation. When skirmishing, independent firing, volleys, and firing a prescribed number of rounds are the methods employed. Whistles are carried by the officers and section N.C.O.'s, but are only used as a caution.

In the attack formation a tendency has been observed on the part of the supports and reserve to close too rapidly upon the skirmishers, thus giving rise to heavy losses.

On the defensive long range fire is avoided, fire being reserved for shorter ranges, *i.e.*, from 600 yards. As the attack develops the reserves move up to the fighting line, and volleys are fired. Independent firing is resorted to when the enemy fixes bayonets. Counter attacks by the reserves upon the enemy's flanks are recommended.

Shelter trenches are much used, one pace per man being reckoned in the firing line, one or two paces per file for the reserves. Parapets 1½ feet thick in sand, 2½ feet in clay soil, are laid down as affording protection from musketry and shrapnel bullets. Profiles are much as in the British service.

Cavalry attacks are met by forming the skirmishers in groups, the reserve in ordinary close formation. Squares are never formed.

Cavalry.—The paces of the Russian cavalry are the walk, 86 yards, the trot, 230 yards, and the gallop, 310 yards a minute.

The squadron is divided into 4 pelotons, each of 16 files: 15 files going to 14 yards, the front of the squadron is about 60 yards. A regiment of 6 squadrons in line occupies a front of 433 yards, including intervals, equal to the front of a peloton, between squadrons.

The principal formations of the squadron are line, columns of pelotons at wheeling distance, and échelon for gaining ground to the front or to a flank by a quarter wheel of pelotons to that flank.

A regiment usually works in line of squadron columns at deploying intervals. The column formations are column of squadrons at wheeling distance, or quarter column (6 yards between squadrons), and columns of pelotons at wheeling distance.

In the attack the general principles are that a reserve is to be provided, depth rather than breadth characterising the formation, and that the attack is to be directed against the flank if possible. Small bodies up to a regiment inclusive, attack in one line, larger bodies in three lines at most.

When acting against cavalry, the front of attacking force should at least equal that of the enemy. The attack trots to within 450 or 600 yards, gallops for 300 or 400 yards, and charges when within 150 yards of the enemy. Against infantry a rapid pace is maintained, the gallop commencing at 800 yards from the enemy. Large bodies of cavalry generally attack in direct échelon of squadrons, the reserve being kept in column. A frequent formation is double échelon of squadrons from the centre, the attack being made by the centre squadrons, the flank squadrons in column of pelotons form the reserve on either flank, 200 or 300 yards in rear.

The Cossack troops have a peculiar formation for attack, known as the "Lava."

In the case of a single squadron acting independently, about half are extended in single rank, with a small detachment, in close order under a special leader (*mayák*) following 50 yards in rear, to serve as a rallying point. The remainder of the squadron, in line or column, forms the reserve some 230 yards in rear. A regiment of 6 squadrons forms 2 "lavas," the first consisting of 3 squadrons, and the second of 2; this latter being drawn up in échelon behind one or both wings of the first; and the remaining squadron, in close order, forms the reserve.

Dismounted tactics are only to be employed as an exception. In a squadron two-thirds of the men of three pelotons dismount, the 4th peloton remaining to act as cavalry; the mounted reserve should never be less than one-fourth the whole. The front of the skirmishing line is 80 to 20 yards per squadron; bayonets are always fixed when dismounted, and tactics follow the same rules as for infantry.

Artillery.—Field batteries (of 8 guns each) are drawn up in line either at full (21 yards), half (9 yards), or close interval (4½ yards), the extent of front of a battery being respectively 147, 65, and 33 yards. Horse artillery, having only 6 guns per battery, 105, 46, and 23 yards respectively.

In action the limbers are about 35 yards in rear of the guns; the ammunition wagons are divided into two lines, the 1st line, consisting of 4 wagons (3 for horse artillery), is placed about 40 yards in rear of the limbers, so that the depth of a battery in action may be taken at 75 yards; the 2nd line, consisting of the remainder of the wagons, is posted 1,100 to 1,200 yards in rear.

Fire, it is laid down, should only be opened at ranges over 3,000 yards for special purposes, such as to make a demonstration, or to attract the attention of the enemy. At long ranges (2,600 to 2,850 yards), and at medium ranges (1,900 to 2,200 yards) either common shell or shrapnel may be used, according to the target; at short ranges (880 to 1,100 yards), common shell only should be employed. An isolated battery, may, on occasion, fire common shell, with one half battery, and shrapnel with the other, in order to produce moral effect, and deceive the enemy as to the number of guns opposed to him. Common shell seems to be preferred to, or at least held of equal value with, shrapnel, but the proportion of the latter in the supply of ammunition slightly exceeds that of the former. It is considered that fire cannot be effective at greater ranges than from 2,680 to 2,850 yards.

At long ranges, to force the enemy to disclose his intentions, and at short ranges, where mobility is required to enable the guns to accompany the infantry, the light field gun is to be preferred, the heavy gun being recommended for medium ranges for the principal artillery struggle. During this struggle it is calculated that a gun would fire two rounds every five minutes, making a round nearly every 19 seconds from a battery of 8 guns, and at this rate the ammunition of a heavy battery would be exhausted in about 4½, a light battery in 6, and a horse artillery battery in 5 hours. It is directed that the fire of common shell or shrapnel over the heads of the troops should often be employed, such fire being continued until the advancing troops interfere with its effect, which it is considered will occur when the troops are within 350 yards of the enemy.

On the offensive, the principle laid down is to get a powerful artillery into position at the commencement of the action, so as to pave the way for the deployment of the infantry, but a portion of the artillery is to be held in reserve at first. Great liberty is given to the artillery in the choice of position, and until the firing line of the infantry deploys, the infantry conform to the movements of the artillery; after the deployment the *rôle* of the infantry is the leading one.

The following is a sketch of the action of artillery when acting on the offensive. 1st zone from 2,800 to 1,700 yards, fire is opened by all the batteries, except those in reserve, to draw the enemy's fire, and get him to disclose his position. The first line of the attacking infantry is 350 to 450 yards in advance of the artillery, the battalion reserve being in line with it. The infantry remains in this position until the attacking artillery has established its superiority, and only moves forward when the guns have to advance to within shorter range. The fire during this period is maintained with deliberation. 2nd zone 1,700 to 800 yards. To enable the artillery to take a decisive part, the guns must be moved forward to within 1,500 to 1,900 yards of the enemy after his artillery fire has been partially subdued. In this new position, the artillery hitherto held in reserve, is generally brought into action. When the enemy's artillery fire has been got under, a brisk fire is directed upon the point of attack, the infantry advances to the attack, the artillery moving forward to support it (changes of position of less than 450 yards are forbidden), if possible to within 800 or 900 yards of the enemy, keeping touch of the battalion reserves. 3rd zone 800 yards and under. A heavy fire is kept up until the object is masked by the attacking infantry. As a rule artillery does not advance nearer to the enemy than 900 yards, but under special circumstances a few batteries may endeavour to advance to within case shot range, to give support to the attack. At the time of the assault, a certain number of batteries are kept limbered up with the 2nd line of the attacking troops to occupy the position if captured, or to cover the retreat in case of repulse.

On the defensive, a certain proportion of the artillery is held in reserve. When the enemy appears within range—say 2,650 yards—the artillery opens fire, and as the attack develops, the reserves are brought into line, to concentrate the fire upon the attacks. If the artillery of the defence is not strong enough to compete with the attack, it should avoid the preliminary duel, so as to preserve its energy for the closer artillery fight.

Fig 5.

Normal order of March.

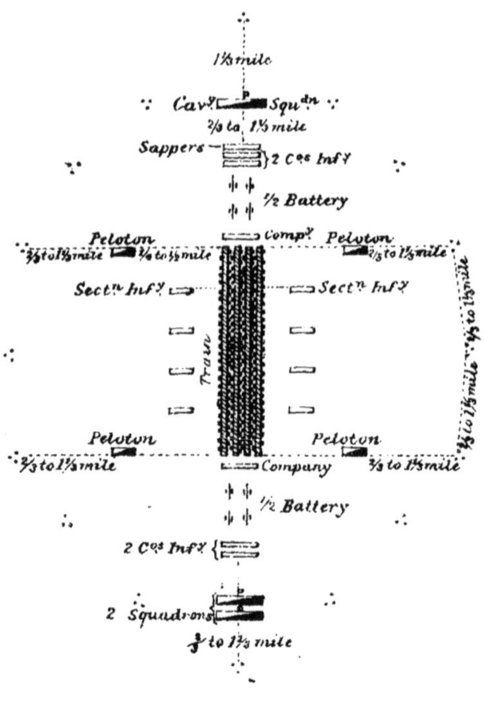

Int: Div: 786(a)

Asiatic Warfare.—The following remarks upon the Russian practice in their steppe campaigns are not without interest.

For operations in Central Asia an extensive train is absolutely necessary for a force of even moderate dimensions, and the protection of that train becomes of such paramount importance that the force itself must act as a mere baggage guard. Hence the movements and disposition of the troops must conform mainly to the rules for the escort of convoys. Moreover, an Asiatic enemy frequently makes his attack from all sides simultaneously, so that front, rear, and flanks have equally to be secured.

An advanced guard, such as is understood by that term in the West, is unnecessary in Asia; but in its place, a peloton, half squadron, or squadron of cavalry is sent out 1 or 1½ miles ahead of the main body, with orders always to keep it in sight. The formation to be adopted by the main body varies in detail according to circumstances; but the accompanying plate (Fig. 5,) which gives the normal order of march for a force, consisting of 2½ battalions (= 10 companies), 4 squadrons and 1 battery, sufficiently indicates the general principles involved. The train of course should march concentrated on as broad a front as possible. If the train consists of vehicles, these are formed in several columns at such intervals as to be able, by a slight wheel, to front to each flank, and so to form a "lager." If the train is composed of animals and vehicles, the former march in the centre, the latter on the flanks, with the same object in view.

In addition to the formed bodies of troops shown in Fig. 5, individual soldiers are posted along the columns of the train as baggage guards.

The length of marches in the steppe depends upon the position of the wells, accordingly distances of from 14 to 30 or even 35 miles may have to be covered. A start should be made as early as possible so as to arrive at the destination before nightfall, and thus give the transport animals time to feed. If, however, the animals have not been able to get a feed before nightfall, they should not start before 6 or 7 a.m. next morning, so that they may be driven out to feed at dawn, and may pick up a little fodder before starting.

As far as possible, marches are made by day, and halts or days of rest are avoided. The former because they shorten the time available in the bivouack; the latter because they tend to prolong the operations, thus necessitating increased supplies and transport. In long marches of from 27 to 33 miles, a halt mid-way is inevitable. The pack animals are then unsaddled.

Bivouacks in the steppe, owing to the necessity of being prepared for an attack from any side, take the form of a "lager" or "zariba," a model of which is given in Fig. 6.

Outpost duty during the day is performed by a few Cossack posts. At night a chain of piquets is thrown out about 280 yards from the lager, each company furnishing two piquets, and the piquets opposite each face being under the orders of the commander of that face. Outlying piquets are also pushed forward on to the most probable lines of hostile approach. A guard under arms is told off to each face of the lager, it having been found by experience to be better to have a guard ready to man each face, than to have one general guard for the whole lager.

Special precautions are taken to prevent a stampede among the animals when grazing. These are as follows: (1) A mounted guard is told off to the herd day and night; (2) Cossack posts are placed round the herd; (3) The horses in the herd are hobbled; (4) The herd is never driven out to pasture till the Cossack posts are in position; (5) and the Cossack posts are not withdrawn till the herd has returned to the lager.

Fig 6.

Normal Lager

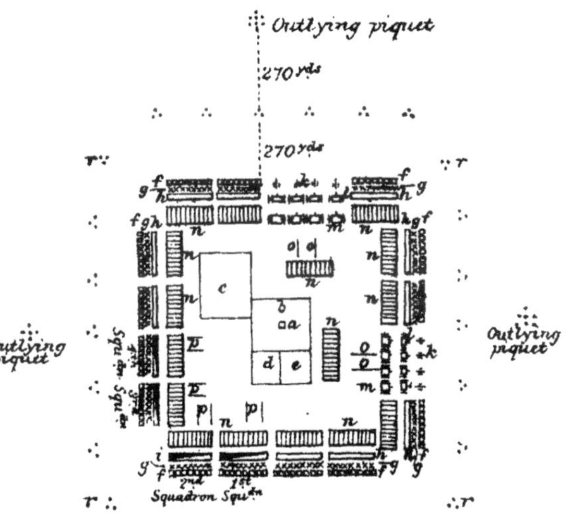

a. Detachment Commander.
b. ——"—— Staff.
c. Hospital.
d. Artillery Park.
e. Engineer —"—
f. Camel packs.
g. Piled Arms.
h. Companies in line.

i. Cossacks.
k. Guns.
l. Limbers.
m. Ammunition Wagons.
n. Camels.
o. Artillery Horse-lines.
p. Cossack ——"——
r. Piquets.

Int: Div 786(6)

CHAPTER IV.

MISCELLANEOUS.

POINTS AS TO WHICH INFORMATION SHOULD BE SOUGHT.

"A straw shows which way the wind blows," "many mickles make a muckle," therefore neglect no scrap of information, however trifling in itself it may appear. Facts based upon personal observation should be carefully distinguished from information derived from rumour. The source of information should always be stated. Great care should be taken to give the date, not only of sending the information, but also the date of the receipt of the information.

The following are briefly the principal points to which attention should be directed.

(*a*.) General.—Position of magazines, arsenals, and depôts, &c. Points of concentration of the army, positions of the army head-quarters and those of the larger units. Strength and composition of the army, and of the various units of the force; quantity of transport present with the troops; names of officers in command of the army, and of the various units. Important positions occupied by the troops. Strength and composition of any reinforcements, whether expected or recently arrived, with dates of arrival or expected arrival. Any changes in position of head-quarters, or of important bodies. Physical condition and appearance of men and horses; condition of clothing and equipment; discipline and spirit of troops.

(*b.*) Troops in camp, quarters or bivouack.—Uniform and distinctive facings, badges, &c., of the troops. Conduct of duties, disposition and strength of outposts, number of tents, bivouack fires; time of despatch, and direction of rounds, patrols, reconnaissances; various signals, and times at which made; collection of materials for fortification, bridging, &c.

(*c.*) Troops on the march.—Strength and composition of each column, its breadth of front and depth, the time each large unit takes to pass a particular point, the rate of marching. Points whence the columns started, direction of march, and destination of the columns. Dates and times of departure. What trains are with the troops. Precautions taken on the line of march.

(*d.*) Troops preparing for action.—The number of lines in which the troops are formed, and their extent; formations adopted by the troops, position of batteries, relative positions of the cavalry and infantry, strength of skirmishing lines; any special concentrations, or turning movements.

(*e.*) Troops retreating.—Traces of men, horses, vehicles, their direction and character. Position and extent of bivouacks, camp fires. Condition of horses abandoned, well-fed or poor, whether with sore backs; character of localities evacuated, to what extent fortified, or devastated; whether bridges, passages, tunnels, &c., have been destroyed.

The Russian Alphabet.

Roman.	Italic.	Equivalents	Roman.	Italic.	Equivalents
А а	*А а*	a	Т т	*ТШ** *т*	t
Б б	*Б б*	b	У у	*У у*	u
В в	*В в*	v [1]	Ф ф	*Ф ф*	f
Г г	*Г г*	g (h) [2]	Х х	*Х х*	kh [8]
Д д	*Д д*	d	Ц ц	*Ц ц*	ts
Е е	*Е е*	e [3]	Ч ч	*Ч ч*	ch [9]
Ж ж	*Ж ж*	j [4]	Ш ш	*Ш ш*	sh
З з	*З з*	z [5]	Щ щ	*Щ щ*	shch [10]
И и	*И и*	i	Ъ ъ	*Ъ ъ*	mute [11]
І і	*І і*	i	Ы ы	*Ы ы*	y [12]
К к	*К к*	k	Ь ь	*Ь ь*	mute [11]
Л л	*Л л*	l	Ѣ ѣ	*Ѣ ѣ*	ye [13]
М м	*М м*	m	Э э	*Э э*	e
Н н	*Н н*	n	Ю ю	*Ю ю*	yu
О о	*О о*	o [6]	Я я	*Я я*	ya
П п	*П п*	p	Ѳ ѳ	*Ѳ ѳ*	th
Р р	*Р р*	r	Ѵ ѵ	*Ѵ ѵ*	i
С с	*С с*	s [7]			

Vowels as in Italian, consonants as in English with following exceptions:—

(1) *ff*, when final. (2) When *g*, as *g* in gate. (3) Pronounce as the word yea when initial. (4) As *z* in azure. (5) As *z* in zenith. (6) As *o* in lock. (7) As *s* in sibyl. (8) As *ch* in loch. (9) As *ch* in church. (10) As combination *shch* in parishchurch. (11) Omit in transliteration. (12) As *y* in lyric. (13) As the word yea.

* This letter is occasionally of this form.

Vocabulary.

The accent shows the syllable upon which the stress falls in pronunciation.

I	ya	my	moï
thou	ty	thy	tvoï
he	on	his	yevó
we	muí	our	nash
you	vuí	your	vash
they	onyí	their	ikh
who?	kto	what?	shto
yes	da	no	nyét
nothing	nichevó	no matter	vsyó ravnó
where	gdyé	here	zdyés
whither	kudá	hither	syudá
whence	otkúda	hence	otsyúda
there	tam	thither	tudá
when	kogdá	now	tepér
how many?	skólko	never	nikogdá

Numerals.

1	odín	18	vosemnádsat
2	dva	19	devyatnádsat
3	tri	20	dvádsat
4	chetýre	21	dvádsat odín
5	pyát	22	dvádsat dva
6	shest	30	trídsat
7	sem	40	sórok
8	vósem	50	pyatdesyát
9	dévyat	60	shestdesyát
10	désyat	70	sémdesyat
11	odínnadsat	80	vósemdesyat
12	dvenádsat	90	devyanósto
13	trinádsat	100	sto
14	chetýrnadsat	101	sto odín
15	pyatnádsat	102	sto dva
16	shestnádsat	200	dvésti
17	semnádsat	300	trísta

400	chetýresta	1000	týsatch
500	pyát sot	2000	dvé týsatchi
600	shest sot		

1st	pérvy	12th	dvenádsaty
2nd	vtorói	20th	dvadsáty
3rd	trétyi	21st	dvádsat pérvy
4th	chetvyórty	22nd	dvádsat vtorói
5th	pyáty	30th	tridsáty
6th	shestói	40th	sorokovói
7th	sedmói	50th	pyatidesyáty
8th	vosmói	90th	devyanósty
9th	devyáty	100th	sóty
10th	desyáty	101st	sto pérvy
11th	odínatsaty	102nd	sto vtorói

Time.

second	sekúnda	Thursday	chetvérg
minute	minúta	Friday	pyátnitsa
hour	chas	Saturday	subbóta
half an hour	polchasá	January	Yanvár
day	dyén	February	Fevrál
week	nedyélia	March	Mart
month	mésyats	April	Aprél
year	god	May	Mái
morning	útro	June	Yun
mid-day	póldyen	July	Yul
evening	vécher	August	Ávgust
night	notch	September	Sentyábr
to-day	sevódnya	October	Octyábr
yesterday	vcherá	November	Noyábr
to-morrow	závtra	December	Dekábr
Sunday	voskresénye	spring	vesná
Monday	ponedyélnik	summer	lyéto
Tuesday	vtórnik	autumn	ósen
Wednesday	sredá	winter	zimá

Points of Compass.

north	séver	east	vostók
south	yug	west	západ

Money.

money	déngi
rouble	rubl (=100 kopeck)*
50 kopeck piece	poltínnik
25 " "	chetverták
20 " "	dvugrívenny
15 " "	pyatialtýnny
10 " "	grívennik
5 " "	pyatatchók

Military Terms.

Ranks.

soldier	soldát
private	ryadovói
lance-corporal	yefreítor
corporal	mládshy unteroffitsér
sergeant	stárshy "
sergeant-major (infantry)	feldvébel
" " (cavalry)	váchmistr
officer	offitsér
sub-lieutenant	podporúchik
lieutenant	porúchik
captain (infantry)	kapitán
" (cavalry)	rótmistr

* The rouble (paper) varies in value according to the rate of exchange; it is now (March, 1890) worth about 2*s.* 1½*d.*

lieut.-colonel	podpolkóvnik
colonel	polkóvnik
major-general	generál mayór
lieut.-general	„ lyeítenant
general	pólny generál

Weapons, &c.

rifle	vintóvka	bayonet	shtyk
cartridge	patrón	bullet	púlya
sword	sháshka	sabre	sáblya
arms	orújye	gun	orúdie
limber	peredók	ammunition wagon	zaryádny yáshchik
powder	pórokh	charge (of gun)	zaryád
projectile	snaryád	common shell	granáta
shrapnel	shrapnél	case shot	kartétch

Troops.

infantry	pekhóta	company	róta
battalion	batalyón	regiment	polk
cavalry	kavalérya	cossack	kazák
squadron	eskadrón	artillery	artilléria
field battery	péshaya battaréya	horse battery	kónnaya battaréya
engineer	injeniér	sapper	sapyór
brigade	brigáda	rifle brigade	strelkóvaya brigáda
division	divísiya	corps	kórpus
army	ármia	staff	shtab

On the March.

to the right	na právo	to the left	na lyévo
forward	vperyód	back	nazád
street	úlitsa	road	doróga
on foot	peshkóm	on horseback	verkhóm

river	reká	stream	ruchéi
bridge	most	ford	brod
hill	gorá	wood	lyés
railway	jelyéznaya doróga	telegraph	telegráf

In Quarters.

town	górod	village	derévnya
church	tsérkoff	house	dom
post-office	pochtóvaya kóntora	hotel	gostínnitsa
governor	gubernátor	police-master	politsimeíster
magistrate	magistrát	official	chinóvnik
village head-man	stárosta	peasant	krestyánin
inhabitant	jítyel	interpreter	perevódchik
hut	izbá	shed	ambár (sarái)
horse	lóshad	cow	koróva
sheep	ovéts	pig	svinyá
fire	ogón	candle	svechá

Provisions, &c.

bread	khlyéb	meat	myáso
beer	pívo	wine	vinó
water	vodá	milk	molokó
tea	chái	coffee	kófe
brandy	vódka	glass	stakán
cup	cháshka	bottle	butýlka
sugar	sákhar	eggs	yáitsa
butter	máslo	cheese	syr
salt	sol	pepper	pérets
hay	séno	straw	solóma
forage	korm	oats	ovyós

please	pojálusta	thank you	blágodaryu vas
have you?	yest li u vas	give us	dáite nam

Useful Abbreviations of Military Terms.

Roman.	Italic.	Equivalent.	Meaning.
Арм.	*арм.*	arméisky	army
Арт.	*арт.*	artillerísky	artillery
Б. Бат.	*б. бат.*	batalyón	battalion
Батар.	*батар.*	bataréya	battery
Бриг.	*бриг.*	brigáda	brígade
Воен. телегр.	*воен. телегр.*	voyénno-telegráfny	military tele-graph
Гв.	*Гв. (гв.)*	gvardiésky	guard
Гор.	*гор.*	górny	mountain (artillery)
Грен.	*грен.*	grenadiérsky	grenadier
Див.	*див. (дuв.)*	divísiya.	division
Драг.	*драг. (драг.)*	dragúnsky	dragoon
Жанд.	*жанд.*	jandármsky	gendarmes
Жел. дор.	*жел. дор.*	jelyéznaya dorógа.	railway
Зап.	*зап.*	zapásny	depôt
Инж.	*инж.*	injenyérny	engineer
Кав.	*кав.*	kavalerísky	cavalry
Каз.	*каз.*	kazáchy	cossack
Кон.	*кон.*	kónny	horse (artil-lery)

USEFUL ABBREVIATIONS OF MILITARY TERMS—*Contd.*

Roman.	Italic.	Equivalent.	Meaning.
Крѣп.	*крѣп.*	krépostny	fortress
Л. Лб.	*л. лб.*	leib	bodyguard
Лтч.	*лтч.*	letúchy	flying (park)
Мѣст.	*мѣст.*	méstny	local
Ор. Оруд.	*ор. оруд. (оруд.)*	orúdie	gun
Ос. Осад.	*ос. осад.*	osádny	siege
П.	*п.*	polk	regiment
Пол.	*пол.*	polevói	field
Понт.	*понт.*	pontónny	pontoon
Пр.	*пр.*	park	park
Птр.	*птр.*	patrónny	cartridge (S.A.A.)
Пѣх.	*пѣх.*	pekhótny	infantry
Пѣш.	*пѣш.*	péshy	field (artillery)
Рез.	*рез.*	rezérvny	reserve
С.	*с.*	sótnia	squadron (Cossack)
Сап.	*сап.*	sapyórny	sapper
Стрѣлк.	*стрѣлк.*	strelkóvy	rifle
Э. Эск.	*эск.*	eskadrón	squadron

Morse Telegraphic Code

Russian.	Equivalent.	Symbol.	Russian.	Equivalent.	Symbol.
А	A	· —	Р	R	· — ·
Б	B	— · · ·	С	S	· · ·
В	V	· — —	Т	T	—
Г	G	— — ·	У	U	· · —
Д	D	— · ·	Ф Ө	F	· · — ·
Е Э	E	·	Х	KH	· · · ·
Ж	J	· · · —	Ц	TS	— · — ·
З	Z	— — · ·	Ч	CH	— — — ·
І И	I	· ·	Ш	SH	— — — —
Й	I	· — — —	Щ	SHCH	— — · —
К	K	— · —	Ъ Ь	MUTE	— · · —
Л	L	· — · ·	Ы	Y	— · — —
М	M	— —	Ѣ	YE	· · — · ·
Н	N	— ·	Ю	YU	· · — —
О	O	— — —	Я	YA	· — · —
П	P	· — — ·			

SPECIAL SYMBOLS.

Imperial Telegram..	· — —
Government „	· — — · · — ·
Service „	· · ·
Private „	— — — ·
Foreign „	— · · — · · —
Calling up „	— · — · —
Commence message	— · · · · — ·
Wait	· — · · ·
Number	— · · — ·
Urgent	— · · · — ·
Words	· · · · — · ·
Midnight to midday	— ·
Midday to midnight	— · ·
Understood...	· · · — ·
Not understood	· · · · · · · · · ·
New line	· — · — · ·
Correction	— · — · — — — · — · ·
End.... ,..	· — · — ·
Receipt	· — · · — · · — ·

Telegraphic numerals and stops as in Western Europe.

Weights and Measures.

Measures of Length.

10 línya = 1 dyúim (English inch).
12 dyúim = 1 fut.
$1\frac{3}{4}$ dyúim = 1 vershók (1·75 inches).
16 vershók = 1 arshín (28 inches).
3 arshín = 1 sajén (7 feet).
500 sajén = 1 verst ($\frac{2}{3}$ mile).

Square Measure.

The square dyúim, arshín, and sajén, are all used, and—

2,400 square sajén = 1 desyatína (2·7 acres).

Dry Goods Measure.

1 gárnets = 2·88 impl. quarts.
8 gárnets = 1 chetverík = 5·77 gallons.
4 chetverík = 1 osmína = 2·88 bushels.
2 osmína = 1 chétvert = 5·77 bushels.

Liquid Measure.

8 shtoff (or 10 krújka) = 1 vedró = 2·7 gallons.

Weights.

96 dólya = 1 zolotník = ·15 oz. (or 65·84 grs. troy).
96 zolotník = 1 funt = ·9 lbs. (or 14·44 oz.).
40 funt = 1 pud = 36·113 lbs.

also used occasionally—

3 zolotník = 1 lot.
10 pud = 1 berkovets.

ORDER OF BATTLE OF THE RUSSIAN FORCES IN ASIA.

TRANSCASPIA.

1st Transcaspian Rifle Brigade

Head-quarters—Askabad.

1st	Transcaspian rifle battalion	Askabad.
2nd	" " "	"
3rd	" " "	"
4th	" " "	"

2nd Transcaspian Rifle Brigade.

Head-quarters—Merv.

5th	Transcaspian rifle battalion	Sarakhs.
6th	" " "	Merv.
7th	" " "	"
8th	" " "	Sari-yazi.

Transcaspian Cossack Cavalry Brigade.

Head-quarters—Askabad.

Taman regiment Kuban Cossacks	Askabad.
Kavkaz " " "	Merv.
Turkoman Militia	"

Artillery.

Head-quarters—Askabad.

4th field battery 20th brigade	Askabad.
3rd " " 21st "	Merv.
6th mountain battery 21st brigade...	Askabad.
4th horse battery Kuban Cossacks	Kakha.

Engineers.

	Transcaspian sapper company	Merv.
1st	" railway battalion...	Kizil-arvat.
2nd	" " "	Charjui.

Fortress and Local Troops see pp. 7, 8.

TURKESTAN.

Turkestan Rifle Brigade.

Head-quarters—Tashkent.

1st	Turkestan rifle battalion	Tashkent.
2nd	" " "	"
3rd	" " "	"
4th	" " "	"

1st Turkestan Frontier Brigade.

Head-quarters—Tashkent.

1st	Turkestan frontier battalion	Tashkent.
10th	" " "	"

2nd Turkestan Frontier Brigade.

Head-quarters—Samarkand.

6th	Turkestan frontier battalion	Samarkand.
8th	" " "	Katty-kurgan.
11th	" " "	Samarkand.
12th	" " "	"
17th	" " "	"

3rd Turkestan Frontier Brigade.

Head-quarters—Margelan.

2nd	Turkestan frontier battalion	Margelan.
4th	" " "	"
7th	" " "	"
15th	" " "	"
16th	" " "	Andijan.
18th	" " "	Kokand.
20th	" " "	Margelan.

4th Turkestan Frontier Brigade.

Head-quarters—Kerki.

3rd	Turkestan frontier battalion	Charjui.
9th	" " "	Kerki.
14th	" " "	"
19th	" " "	"

Unattached.

5th Turkestan frontier battalion	Petro-alexandrovsk.
13th " " "	"

Cavalry.

4th Orenburg Cossack regiment	Petro-alexandrovsk.
5th " " "	Tashkent.
6th " " "	Margelan.
2nd Ural " "	Samarkand.
Astrakhan Cossacks (2 squadrons)	Kerki.

Turkestan Artillery Brigade.

Head-quarters—Tashkent.

1st Turkestan (field) battery	Samarkand.
2nd " " "	Tashkent.
3rd " " "	Margelan.
4th " " "	Kerki.
5th " " "	Tashkent.
6th " " "	Samarkand.
7th " (mountain) battery	"

Unattached Batteries.

2nd Orenburg Cossack horse battery	Samarkand.
Turkestan mountain horse "	Margelan.

Engineers.

Turkestan sapper half battalion	Tashkent.

Fortress and Local Troops see page 11.

OMSK.

West Siberian Frontier Brigade.

Head-quarters—Verny.

3rd West Siberian frontier battalion	Djarkent
5th " " "	Verny.
6th " " "	"
7th " " "	"
8th " " "	Kopal.

Unattached.

1st West Siberian frontier battalion	Semipalatinsk.
4th " " "	Zaisansk.

Cavalry.

1st Siberian Cossack regiment	Djarkent.
2nd " "	Borokhudzir.
3rd " "	Zaisansk.
1st Semirechia Cossack regiment	Verny.

West Siberian Artillery Brigade.

Head-quarters—Verny.

1st West Siberian (field) battery	Verny.
2nd " " "	Djarkent.
3rd " (mountain) battery	Karakol.
4th " (field) battery	Zaisansk.
West Siberian mountain horse battery	Ust-kamenogorsk.

Engineers.

West Siberian sapper company	Verny.

Reserve Troops.

Tobolsk reserve cadre battalion	Tobolsk.
Tomsk " "	Tomsk.
Omsk " "	Omsk.
Semipalatinsk reserve cadre battalion	Semipalatinsk.

Reserve Cavalry, see page 14.

Local Troops, see page 15.

IRKUTSK.

Irkutsk reserve cadre battalion	Irkutsk.
Krasnoyarsk reserve cadre battalion	Krasnoyarsk.
Irkutsk Cossack squadron	Irkutsk.
Krasnoyarsk Cossack squadron	Krasnoyarsk.

Local Troops, see page 17.

PRI-AMUR.

1st East Siberian Rifle Brigade.

Head-quarters—Nikolskoe.

1st East Siberian rifle battalion	Razdolnoe.
2nd " "	Anuchino.
3rd " "	Nikolskoe.
4th " "	"
5th " "	Unposted.

2nd East Siberian Rifle Brigade.

Head-quarters—Novokievskoe.

6th East Siberian rifle battalion	Novgorodsky.
7th " " "	Slavianka.
8th " " "	Barabash.
9th " " "	Novokievskoe.
10th " " "	Unposted.

Frontier Battalions.

1st East Siberian frontier battalion...	Vladivostok.
2nd " " "	Blagovesh-chensk.
3rd " " "	Khabarovka.
4th " " "	Troitskosavsk.
5th " " "	Vladivostok.
2nd West " " "	"

Cossack Infantry.

1st Transbaikal Cossack battalion	Chita.
2nd " " "	Kara convict works.
Amur Cossack half battalion	Ekaterino-nikolskaya.
Ussurian Cossack half battalion	Kamen Ry-balov.

Cavalry.

1st Ussurian horse squadron	Atamanovskoe.
2nd " "	Khunchun.
1st Transbaikal Cossack regiment	Chita.
Amur Cossack regiment	Blagovesh-chensk.

East Siberian Artillery Brigade.

Head-quarters—Nikolskoe.

1st East Siberian (field) battery*	Blagoveshchensk.
2nd " " "	Nikolskoe.
3rd " (mountain) "	Novokievskoe.
4th " " "	Barabash.
1st Transbaikal Cossack horse battery	Verkhneudinsk.
2nd " " " "	Chita.

Engineers.

East Siberian Sapper Company	Vladivostok.

Reserve Troops.

Strétinsk reserve Cadre battalion	Strétinsk.

Reserve Cossack Formations, see page 21.
Local and Fortress Troops, see pp. 22, 23.

* The mountain section of this battery is at Khabarovka.

DISTRIBUTION OF THE RUSSIAN FORCES IN ASIA.*

TRANSCASPIA.

Askabad	Head-quarters 1st Transcaspian rifle brigade. 1st, 2nd, 3rd, 4th Transcaspian rifle battalions. 4th (field) battery, 20th artillery brigade. 6th (mountain) battery, 21st artillery brigade. Head-quarters Transcaspian cavalry brigade. Taman regiment of Kuban Cossacks. Askabad fortress artillery company. Askabad local detachment (365)
Charjui†	...2nd Transcaspian railway battalion.
Kakha	...4th horse battery Kuban Cossacks.
Kizil-arvat	...1st Transcaspian railway battalion.
Merv	Head-quarters 2nd Transcaspian rifle brigade. 6th, 7th Transcaspian rifle battalions. 3rd (field) battery, 21st artillery brigade. Kavkaz regiment of Kuban Cossacks. Turkoman Militia. Transcaspian sapper company. Merv local detachment (186).
Sarakhs	5th Transcaspian rifle battalion. Sarakhs local detachment (244).
Sari-yazi	...8th Transcaspian rifle battalion.

TURKESTAN.

Andijan	...16th Turkestan frontier battalion.
Charjui‡	3rd Turkestan frontier battalion. Charjui local detachment (202).
Katty-kurgan	8th Turkestan frontier battalion. Katty-kurgan local detachment (215).

* Those places are omitted at which only local troops are quartered.
† See also under Turkestan.
‡ See also under Transcaspia.

Kerki	Head-quarters 4th Turkestan frontier brigade. 9th, 14th, 19th Turkestan frontier battalions. 2 squadrons Astrakhan Cossacks. 4th Turkestan field battery.
Kokand	...18th Turkestan frontier battalion.
Margelan	Head-quarters 3rd Turkestan frontier brigade. 2nd, 4th, 7th, 15th, 20th Turkestan frontier battalions. 6th Orenburg Cossack regiment. 3rd Turkestan field battery. Turkestan mountain horse battery.
Petro-Alexandrovsk	5th, 13th Turkestan frontier battalions. 4th Orenburg Cossack regiment.
Samarkand	Head-quarters 2nd Turkestan frontier brigade. 6th, 11th, 12th, 17th Turkestan frontier battalions. 2nd Ural Cossack regiment. 1st, 6th (field), 7th (mountain) Turkestan batteries. 2nd Orenburg Cossack horse battery. Fortress artillery company.
Tashkent	Head-quarters Turkestan rifle brigade. 1st, 2nd, 3rd, 4th Turkestan rifle battalions. Head-quarters 1st Turkestan frontier brigade. 1st, 10th Turkestan frontier battalions. 5th Orenburg Cossack regiment. Head-quarters, and 2nd, 5th field batteries Turkestan artillery brigade. Turkestan sapper half battalion. Fortress artillery company.

OMSK.

Borokhudzir	2nd Siberian Cossack regiment. Borokhudzir local detachment (106).
Djarkent	3rd West Siberian frontier battalion. 1st Siberian Cossack regiment. 2nd West Siberian field battery.
Karakol*	3rd West Siberian mountain battery. Karakol local detachment (300).
Kopal	8th West Siberian frontier battalion. Kopal local detachment (283).
Omsk	...Omsk reserve cadre battalion.
Semipalatinsk	1st West Siberian frontier battalion. Semipalatinsk reserve cadre battalion.
Tobolsk	...Tobolsk reserve cadre battalion.
Tomsk	...Tomsk reserve cadre battalion.
Ust-kamenogorsk	West Siberian mountain horse battery. Ust-kamenogorsk local detachment (335).

* This place has recently been renamed Prejevalsk.

Verny	Head-quarters West Siberian frontier brigade. 5th, 6th, 7th West Siberian frontier battalions. 1st Semirechia Cossack regiment. Head-quarters and 1st field battery West Siberian artillery brigade. West Siberian sapper company.
Zaisansk	4th West Siberian frontier battalion. 3rd Siberian Cossack regiment. 4th West Siberian field battery. Zaisansk local detachment (180).

IRKUTSK.

Irkutsk	Irkutsk reserve cadre battalion. Irkutsk Cossack squadron.
Krasnoyarsk	Krasnoyarsk reserve cadre battalion. Krasnoyarsk Cossack squadron.

PRI-AMUR.

Anuchino	...2nd East Siberian rifle battalion.
Atamanovskoe	...1st Ussurian horse squadron.
Barabash	8th East Siberian rifle battalion. 4th East Siberian mountain battery.
Blagovesh-chensk.	2nd East Siberian frontier battalion. Amur Cossack cavalry regiment. 1st East Siberian field battery.
Chita	1st Transbaikal Cossack battalion. 1st Transbaikal Cossack cavalry regiment. 2nd Transbaikal Cossack horse battery. Chita local detachment (104).
Ekaterino-nikolskaya	Amur Cossack half battalion.
Kamen-Rybalov	Ussurian Cossack half battalion.
Kara convict works	2nd Transbaikal Cossack battalion.
Khabarovka	3rd East Siberian frontier battalion. 1st East Siberian battery (mountain section).
Khunchun	...2nd Ussurian horse squadron.
Nikolaievsk	Nikolaievsk local detachment (228). Nikolaievsk fortress artillery company (104).

Nikolskoe	Head-quarters 1st East Siberian rifle brigade. 3rd, 4th East Siberian rifle battalions. Head-quarters and 2nd field battery East Siberian artillery brigade.
Novgorodsky	...6th East Siberian rifle battalion.
Novokievskoe	Head-quarters 2nd East Siberian rifle brigade. 9th East Siberian rifle battalion. 3rd East Siberian mountain battery.
Razdolnoe	...1st East Siberian rifle battalion.
Slavianka	...7th East Siberian rifle battalion.
Strétinsk	...Strétinsk reserve cadre battalion.
Troitskosavsk	...4th East Siberian frontier battalion.
Verkhneudinsk	1st Transbaikal Cossack horse battery. Verkhneudinsk local detachment (133).
Vladivostok	1st, 5th East Siberian frontier battalions. 2nd West Siberian frontier battalion. East Siberian sapper company. 1st and 2nd fortress artillery companies (678).
Unposted	...5th, 10th East Siberian rifle battalions.

STRENGTH OF THE RUSSIAN FORCES IN ASIA.

		Field Troops.					Reserve Troops.			Railway Troops.	Local Troops		Grand Total.	
		Infantry.	Cavalry.	Artillery.	Engineers.	Total.	Infantry.	Cavalry.	Artillery.		Infantry.	Artillery.	Men.	Guns.
Transcaspia	peace	6,818	2,325	945	288	10,376	—	—	—	2,124	1,522	115	14,137	30
	war ...	8,321	2,325	1,014	288	11,948	—	—	—	2,124	1,522	115	15,709	30
Turkestan	peace ...	18 022	3,074	2,345	525	23,966	—	—	—	—	2,583	448	26,997	64
	war ...	25,038	3,074	2,492	525	31,129	—	—	—	—	2,583	448	34,190	68
Omsk	peace ...	5,229	3,716	962	159	10,066	2,896	—	—	—	6,273	—	19,235	34
	war	7,245	3,716	1,198	279	12,438	11,928	7,432	—	—	6,641	—	38,412	38
Irkutsk	peace ...	—	242	—	—	242	2,122	—	—	—	1,292	—	3,656	—
	war ...	—	242	—	—	242	8,097	—	—	—	1,292	—	9,631	—
Pri-amur	peace ...	18,729	1,768	1,326	260	22,083	555	—	—	—	2,286	782	25,706	40
	war ...	19,716	2,287	1,704	260	23,967	8,596	1,946	271	—	2,286	782	37,848	50
Total	peace ...	48,798	11,125	5,578	1,232	66,733	5,573	—	—	2,124	13,956	1,345	89,731	168
	war	60,320	11,644	6,408	1,352	79,724	28,621	9,378	271	2,124	14,297	1,345	135,760	186

SYNOPTICAL TABLE OF UNIFORMS.

Colour of uniform.	Shoulder-strap.			Cap-band.			Troops.
	Colour.	Piping.	Insignia.	Colour.	Piping.	Insignia.	
Green ...	Scarlet... ...	Nil. ...	Letters (p. 24)... ...	Scarlet... ...	Nil ...	Letters (p. 24) ...	Reserve infantry.
" ...	"	" ...	*C* (p. 27)	"	" ...	Nil	Siberian Cossacks.
" ...	"	" ..	No. or letters (p. 30)...	Black	Scarlet	Number (p. 30) ...	Field artillery.
" ...	"	" ...	Letters (p. 33)... ...	"	"	Nil	Fortress artillery.
" ...	"	" ..	Letters (p. 32)	Green	"	"	Mountain horse artillery.
" ...	"	" ...	Letters (p. 35)	"	"	Letters (p. 35) ...	Engineers.
" ...	Crimson ...	" ...	No. and letter (p. 27)	Crimson ...	Nil ...	Nil	Semirechia Cossacks.
" ...	" ...	" ...	No. and letters (p. 24)	Green	Crimson	No. and letters (p. 24)	Rifle battalions
" ...	Blue	" ...	No. and letters (p. 24)	Scarlet... ...	Nil ...	No. and letters (p. 24)	Frontier battalions.
" ...	"	yellow	Number (pp. 27, 32) ...	Blue	Yellow	Nil	Orenburg Cossacks.
" ...	Green	scarlet	Nil	Green	Scarlet	M.	Local troops.
" ...	"	yellow	No. and letters (pp. 27, 31).	"	Yellow	Nil	Ussurian or Amur Cossacks.
" ...	Yellow... ...	Nil.	No. and letters (pp. 24, 27, 32).	Yellow ...	Nil ...	"	Irkutsk, Krasnoyarsk, Transbaikal Cossacks.
Blue ...	Crimson ...	" ...	Number (p. 27) ...	Crimson ...	"	"	Ural Cossacks.
" ...	Yellow... ...	" ...	Number (p. 27) ...	Yellow... ...	"	"	Astrakhan Cossacks.
Brown ...	Scarlet... ...	" ...	Letter (pp. 27, 32) ...	Scarlet... ...	"	"	Kuban Cossacks.

www.ingramcontent.com/pod-product-compliance
Ingram Content Group UK Ltd.
Pitfield, Milton Keynes, MK11 3LW, UK
UKHW021835270726
14058UKWH00002B/167

9 781847 348593